W9-COF-048

FROM BARTER TO BANKING:
THE STORY OF MONEY

FROM BARTER

TO BANKING:

THE STORY OF MONEY

BY WILLIAM W. WADE

CROWELL-COLLIER PRESS   *New York*
COLLIER-MACMILLAN LIMITED   *London*

Library of Congress Catalog Card Number: 67–19956
The Macmillan Company, New York
Collier-Macmillan Canada Ltd., Toronto, Ontario
Printed in the United States of America
FIRST PRINTING

PICTURE CREDITS:

Bank of New York (page 48); The Bettmann Archive, Inc.
(page 95); Black Star (page 100); Brown Brothers (pages 3,
79, 83, 116); Bureau of the Mint (pages 30, 42); Chase Manhattan Bank Money Museum (title pages, facing page 1, and
pages 6–7, 10–12, 15, 16, 20–22, 24, 59, 108–109, 113); Culver
Pictures, Inc. (pages 18, 51, 60–61, 65, 74); Ezra Stoller Asso-
ciates (page 122); Federal Reserve Bank of New York (page
129); U. S. Treasury Department (page 37).

CONTENTS

FROM BARTER TO BANKING:
THE STORY OF MONEY

All kinds of things
have been used for money.

INTRODUCTION

SOMEWHERE, SOMETIME in the unrecorded past man invented money. We can guess that a group of men were involved, since the idea of money has to be accepted by more than one man before the money is of any use. It was a social invention in the interest of convenience and efficiency, just as the invention of language and the creation of new words are the acts of men and women and children living together. We can also guess that the first money consisted of shells, bones, glittering stones, hides, or some similar portable objects, for all kinds of things have been used for money in ancient societies. But while we guess about these origins, we know about the importance of the invention—the step it meant toward civilized life.

Money is one of civilization's most important tools. We could not do without it without changing modern life in a fundamental way. Barter—swapping one thing for another—simply would not work in our age of jet planes, nuclear power, and space exploration. An enterprising boy can swap his wagon for a toy truck, the truck for a slingshot, and the slingshot for what he really wanted in the first place, a pocket knife. We can imagine a farmer swapping poultry and vegetables for the services of a doctor or the work of a mechanic to fix the farmer's tractor. But today we have, and we need, so many kinds of specialists, it would be a hopeless and endless task to barter their work and their skills in exchange for the many products and services they might need or want. Without the magic of money, how could we pay the men who explore the deserts for the crude oil to refine into gasoline to drive our cars? How could we reward the research scientist, the world's musicians, the men who build highways, telephone operators, university professors, novelists, television actors, diplomats, sea captains, coal miners? Money isn't everything, as the saying goes, but it plays a part in most human endeavors—in a soldier's pay, in the building of a hospital, in the offering plate at church. It brings coffee to our shores from Brazil, tea from India, Volkswagens from Germany, and cameras from Japan. It can be spent in a thousand delightful ways. It can be squandered or hoarded, invested, lost, given away, wasted, or treated wisely. Some men earn it slowly by great effort; a few seem to attract it to themselves miraculously. It has led men to cheat and murder and steal—and it has also led them to be wonderfully creative.

Money cannot only be managed or mismanaged by individuals. Whole nations can develop money troubles and find themselves in collective misery. In fact, in the 1920's and the 1930's money troubles galloped across national frontiers and resulted in a world depression that brought trade to a standstill, closed banks, wiped out fortunes, wrenched farmers from their lands, and threw people out of work by the millions. The economic depression of the 1930's contributed to the rise of Hitler and Mussolini, the strengthening of communism, and the coming of World War II. And money played a part in winning the war, as the economic strength of America was mobilized as the arsenal of democracy. After the war, too,

The New York Stock Exchange during the Wall Street Crash of 1929.

money was called upon, under the Marshall Plan, to help rebuild Europe. Today it is used to help underdeveloped nations in their struggle against poverty and in their search for the rising living standards enjoyed by industrial countries.

Money, then, has a large place in modern history. It is something more than a pocketful of dimes and quarters and a few folded bills waiting to be spent. It has its influence on how people choose and pursue their vocations; it helps shape our nation and our world. And almost all of us are fascinated by ideas of how we might acquire more of it, and most of us can be quickly befuddled and bewildered when we try to follow the intricacies of how and when and why the Treasury issues money and how the government regulates the banking system so vital to the flow of money.

Fascinating, befuddling, money is one of man's social inventions worthy of more study and understanding.

1 / WAMPUM, DRACHMAS, AND GREENBACKS

MONEY HAS BEEN important to the process of civilization and it may well have been invented more than once. It has certainly developed in different ways in various parts of the world. As we all know, the European explorers who came to the New World found that the Indians exchanged goods for wampum made of beads laboriously fashioned out of shells. Early voyagers into the interior of Ethiopia reported that the people used blocks of salt for money. Traders touching the Pacific island of Yap found one of the world's heaviest forms of money—huge round stones fifty pounds or more in weight with a hole in the middle so they could be mounted on poles to be carried. And elsewhere in the Pacific—in the New Hebrides—people have used one of the lightest of monies—the feathers of birds.

With this rich variety of evidence, historians seeking the origin of money can piece together interesting theories. Some suggest that one of our ancient ancestors in-

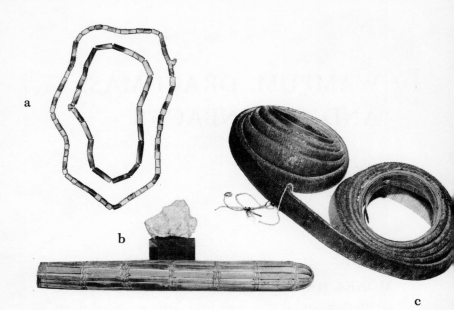

a

b

c

vented money when he bartered an animal hide or a sack of grain for a stone axe or arrowhead he didn't need at the moment. The fact that he did not need the axe or arrowhead is important. For this early trader, so the theory goes, wanted to use the tools he received not for themselves but as something to trade at a later time for food or clothing. He wanted to use them as a medium of exchange, as money. And he acted on the assumption that his fellowmen would accept these stone age tools in some future transaction.

This is guesswork, of course. But those who suggest this theory of "tool money" note that archeologists have found vast hoards of both arrowheads and axes along with the remains of ancient men in several places in Europe. The historians say these hoards may have been primitive

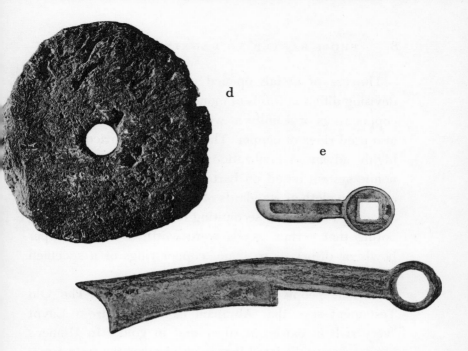

d

e

Money has developed in different ways in various parts of the world: (a) Indian wampum, (b) African salt money, (c) a feather-coated strip from the New Hebrides, (d) a Yap Island stone, and (e) Chinese copper knife money.

banks. And they point out that some of the axes and other tools in these collections were too small and delicate for actual use, that they were symbols rather than real articles.

In ancient China, too, there is similar evidence. The Chinese learned to work with copper as early as 2300 B.C. By the seventh century before Christ, and probably much earlier, they were making tiny copper plates shaped like hoes, spades, swords, and knives and using them as money.

The use of metals opened up new opportunities for devising different forms of money. The Chinese developed copper rings of a uniform weight. In time the Egyptians also used rings of copper. The Egyptians carried on their highly advanced civilization for centuries with an economic system based on barter. They used sacks of corn and linen cloth as standards of exchange. They developed a complex system of accounting for business transactions, noting that certain goods were worth so many copper bowls or dishes or so many copper rings of a specified weight.

Ancient people set values in many ways. The Old Testament says that Abraham came back from Egypt "very rich in cattle, in silver and in gold." In Homer's Greece, men calculated the worth of other things in terms of oxen. Cattle and goats have been a form of wealth and have served as units of accounting in Africa and many other parts of the world both in antiquity and relatively recent times. In Ceylon at one time men reckoned values in terms of elephants, which must have made it difficult to buy something small or to make change. An elephant economy has all kinds of disadvantages. A rich man, for instance, faced the hazard of being trampled by his wealth.

It was the need to make trading easier that gave rise to better forms of money. And the eastern rim of the Mediterranean Sea, where men journeyed back and forth and exchanged goods in increasing quantities, was a place

where the necessity was particularly strong. Here too in
the seventh century before Christ, there was growing
wealth and legends about it. King Midas, it is said, was
given the golden touch, a gift that almost caused him to
starve until the gods consented to take it back. According
to the story, Midas lost his power to transform objects into
gold by bathing in the Pactolus River, in what is now
Turkey, and the stones in the river thereby turned into
gold. It was in Western Turkey that the Kingdom of Lydia
flourished some seven hundred years before Christ. One
of the last of these Lydian kings was Croesus whose
treasures of gold and jewels were famous throughout the
classical world. To be as rich as Croesus was to be wealthy
beyond one's dreams. Fittingly, Croesus had among his
riches the world's first coins.

These coins were cast either by the Lydians themselves
or by neighboring Greeks who were allied with them.
They were made of electrum, a mixture of gold and
silver. For some time precious metals had been used in
trade. And craftsmen, using tools of bronze and iron, had
learned to stamp them to designate weight and purity.
The first coins had a design on one side and a relatively
crude stamp on the other. An electrum coin of King
Croesus' time shows a lion and a bull facing each other,
with an indented square on the reverse. Croesus, in keeping with his reputation, was the first monarch to issue
coins of pure gold.

The Greeks brought all their wonderful artistic talents

A Lydian electrum stater (700–637 B.C.).

to coin making; their money became widely used throughout the Mediterranean world and is still being discovered and collected today. One of their most famous coins was known as the Attic owl, with the head of Athene, the goddess of wisdom, on one side and a common Grecian owl on the other. It was a tetradrachm, that is, four drachmas. It was a coin of high value, for it was said that a man's yearly income might amount to thirty tetradrachms. Drachma literally means a handful and may originally have referred to a handful of nails. And so we can assume that at one time a tetradrachm bought four handfuls of nails and that nails were expensive in the days of the Greeks.

Another famous coin was a tetradrachm that was struck under the reign of Alexander the Great. On one side it had the head of Heracles—or Hercules, as the Romans later called him—and on the other side the seated figure of Zeus holding an eagle and a thunderbolt. This coin circulated throughout Alexander's empire and continued to be issued for more than two centuries after his death. Alexander also issued a gold coin with the head of Athene

A Greek tetradrachm showing the Attic owl and the head of Athene (525–430 B.C.).

as pictured by the famous sculptor Phidias. These are only a few of the rich variety of Greek coins that passed from hand to hand in the ancient world. Stores of them have turned up in such distant places as Spain, Egypt, and Great Britain in relatively recent years.

The Greco-Roman civilization was a great one and it is natural that both the uses and abuses of money flourished while it lasted. Counterfeiting, for instance, was common enough; it occurred almost as soon as the first coins appeared. The Greek historian Herodotus, who lived during the sixth century before Christ, wrote about soldiers who were paid with coins made of lead and coated with a thin golden case. Greek city officials in 400 B.C. held meetings to agree on standards for their coins and to establish a death penalty for any officer found guilty of debasing the metal used in money. In Rome a counterfeiter could be thrown into the arena with starving lions or he could be hanged. An informer who helped trap him could be exempted from taxes or, if a slave, be given his freedom. It is plain enough, then, that desperate deeds were sometimes done for money.

Roman coins: (left) a bronze
follis (A.D. 35–353); (right) a
denarius (A.D. 14–37).

The first Roman coins were awkward, bulky pieces of
bronze weighing a pound. But the Romans soon found
that money was vital to the organization of government
and they developed it with their own efficiency. They set
up a number of official mints under the control of the
Roman Senate and with special officers designated to buy
silver bullion. New silver coins were issued in 268 B.C.
and were used, among other things, for paying troops in
scattered places. The most famous Roman denomination
was the denarius, which is roughly equivalent to our
dollar. The denarius was worth four sesterces. The
Romans reckoned their higher values in talents, a measure
used in still earlier times. A talent was worth six thousand
denarii, but a talent was only a measure, not a coin or unit
of currency.

During the Roman Republic the Senate had control
of coining money. As time went on, individual generals

began issuing their own money to pay their troops, and this was an important factor in the struggle for power just before the beginning of the Christian calendar. One of these generals was Julius Caesar who struck a coin showing an elephant trampling a serpent to commemorate his conquest of Gaul. When Caesar became emperor he broke the Roman tradition of depicting only gods, mythical figures, and dead heroes on coins. He issued a denarius with his own likeness on it—the first living Roman to be so honored. But the distinction lasted only a short time. Within a month he was assassinated.

During the time of Christ many kinds of money circulated in the Holy Land and historians have puzzled over some of the forms mentioned in the Bible. They think that the widow's mite was a small copper or bronze coin of little value, possibly one cast by Pontius Pilate showing three stalks of grain on one side and a wine ladle on the other. The thirty pieces of silver paid to Judas for his act of betrayal are a matter of guesswork. The experts think they were tetradrachms of Greek or Phoenician origin. The thirty coins were enough for Judas to buy a piece of land, and the Roman denarius was not valuable enough for that.

Money was tampered with not only by people outside the law in Roman times but by the government themselves. What we now call inflation—the decline in the value of money as measured by the amount of goods it will buy—was quite a normal occurrence during some periods. Costly wars, the need to pay soldiers on long and distant expeditions of conquest, times of government instability and strife—all contributed to the debasing of coinage and falling public confidence in existing money. The Roman emperors that followed Caesar and his successor, Caesar Augustus, began making coins of gold and silver that were less and less pure. A ruler named Diocletian issued a bronze coin with only a thin layer of silver and people had so little confidence in this kind of money that they began to carry large bags of it around to exchange for whatever goods they could buy. Constantine, the emperor who moved his capital to Constantinople and who instituted many reforms, had to find a new coin too. This was the solidus, or besant, a coin which, because it was made of gold, was used and valued for seven hundred years. The solidus became the model for later British, Spanish, French, and Swedish coins.

Able rulers like Constantine and his descendant, Justinian, tended to have sound monetary systems. But when empires weakened, when nomadic barbarians moved in, warring and plundering, then established economic relationships were replaced by force of arms. Sometimes a barbarian chieftain tried to take over parts of the Roman Empire and rule it as the Romans did—with law, taxation, and established pay for his soldiers. But the temptation of his lieutenants to revolt and to sustain their own power by promising their followers greater plunder was usually too strong. After long years of anarchic warring, the feudal societies of the Middle Ages developed a military and economic organization of their own, more de-

A Byzantine solidus
(A.D. 641–668).

centralized than the Roman Empire and more reliant on barter than on money. Men who tilled the soil—vassals, serfs, and peasants—paid rent in kind; that is, they gave either farm goods or so many days of labor each year to the lord who owned or managed the land on which the farmers lived. Custom and tradition—not bargaining or the existence of a market—set the amounts the serf, the lord, and the church should have. Under the feudal military system, the peasantry provided a rough soldiery, but the lords provided an efficient armored cavalry, leadership, and courage—in short, protection. And it was in the feudal times that the Crusades, those long, adventurous expeditions to liberate the Holy Land from the Turks, were begun. It is interesting that one of the first crusaders was known as Walter the Pennyless. It was an era of history when commerce was declining and money was not highly prized.

At about the same time in a far eastern part of the world there was a ruler who had developed a new monetary system—and a European merchant to take note of

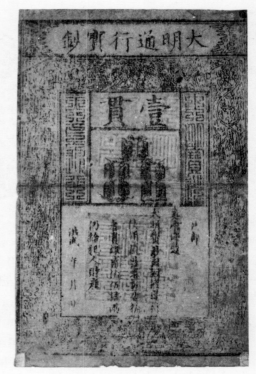

The Chinese made paper from the bark of the mulberry tree, cutting it into different sizes for different denominations of money. This fourteenth-century specimen of paper currency used in the Mongolian Empire is as big as a sheet of typing paper.

this. The place was China; the ruler Kublai Khan; the merchant Marco Polo. Marco Polo reported that the economic development under Kublai had reached astonishing proportions. The khan had restored a grand canal, improved imperial roads, and established a postal service using two hundred thousand horses. He also provided charitable relief for orphans, the sick and the aged and set up a system to inspect and purchase crops to be stored until times of famine. What was even more amazing, the khan was using, of all things, money made of paper. Marco Polo told how the paper was made from the bark of the mulberry tree, cut into different sizes for different denominations. "The coinage of this paper money," he wrote, "is authenticated with as much form and ceremony as if it were actually of pure gold or silver. . . . The act of counterfeiting is punished as a capital offense. . . . This paper currency is circulated in every part of the grand khan's dominions; nor dares any person, at peril of his life, refuse to accept it in payment. All his subjects receive it without hesitation, because, wherever their business may call them, they can dispose of it again in the purchase of merchandise they may have occasion for; such as pearls, jewels, gold or silver. With it, in short, every article may be procured."

But the khan's fabulous money, sound as it was at the time Marco Polo observed it, had a relatively short reign —only fifty years or so. Although based on silver and printed in limited amounts at first, the temptation to issue more and more was very great. And the more that was issued, the less people valued it. Before long new money had to be made to replace the old on a five-for-one basis. Then, after another interval of depreciation, the whole thing was repeated again. Shortly after 1300, as the khan's empire itself was weakening, its paper money became a historical curiosity.

Europeans of the fifteenth century, although interested in trade and travel and stirring from the economic stagnation of the Middle Ages, read Marco Polo's account, but continued to use coins and precious metals for their money. Some of their coins were highly valued, others fell into disrepute. In England during the early sixteenth cen-

Sir Thomas Gresham described the principle that "bad money drives out good."

tury, Henry VIII experimented with the profitable, for him, practice of debasing the coinage. He issued a coin of one-third silver and two-thirds copper. One side of the coin was stamped with his image and unfortunately a little wear soon gave it a red nose. Henry became known as "Old Copper Nose." At this time Gresham's law was developed by Sir Thomas Gresham, a merchant and financier and founder of the English Royal Exchange, who described the principle that "bad money drives out good." This means that when a person has two coins, one of pure metal and the other with Henry's copper nose showing through, he will spend the one of lesser value and hoard the other. Given enough bad money, the bad will be the only kind that circulates.

In this era, too, Europeans were learning something about the relationship of money and national power. The

Spanish conquistadores roamed the New World looking for treasure, supported and supplied by rulers who needed additional wealth to maintain and expand their empires. When Pizarro invaded the realm of the Incas he found them using fabulous amounts of gold not as money but as decoration. Sheets of it covered their buildings, and their craftsmen had molded it into life-sized statues of llamas and fields of finely made ears of corn and grain. Eyewitnesses have said that the workmanship was exquisite but little has survived. It was all melted down by the invaders, to be cast into coins of the European powers and to be fought over in Europe's wars.

This was the money that also circulated in North America as it was being explored and settled. One common silver coin, about the size of our present silver dollar, was the Spanish peso. It was worth eight smaller monetary units—"reales"—and stamped with a large eight on one side. These were the pieces of eight of the days of piracy. People used to break them into halves or quarters to make change. A quarter of the coin was worth two reales, or "two bits"; a half was worth "four bits." And this is where we get our present slang for 25-cent and 50-cent pieces.

Young America had cosmopolitan money—British guineas, Bermuda "hogs" showing a pig, Portuguese halfjoes. It also had a good deal of homemade money. In Virginia and other southern states tobacco was the main medium of exchange for many years. Nails, bullets, and furs were also used. In Canada a French colonial governor

Cosmopolitan coins from the Colonial period: (a) a British guinea, (b) a Bermuda "hog," and (c) a Portuguese half-joe.

found he couldn't pay his soldiers because a shipment of silver failed to arrive. When the soldiers objected, he seized all playing cards and ordered that cards bearing his signature should be honored as money. This worked well, so well that when the silver arrived the paper money continued to circulate and the silver was stored away as backing for the newer form.

But paper money again proved a little too convenient. Massachusetts tried issuing some in 1690 and other colonies did the same. In all cases either there was too much counterfeiting or the issuing governments failed to support it with sufficient backing to maintain public confidence. Paper money passed out of use until the American Revolution. The Continental Congress found the public treasury empty and so it tried paper money once more. Paul Revere engraved the bills. But *because* the public treasury was empty, Americans were soon describing useless objects as "not worth a Continental." By the end of the war one hundred Continental dollars were only worth a single silver Spanish dollar.

After the war, the young United States relied mainly

Goods sold to the Indians were often priced in beaver skins.

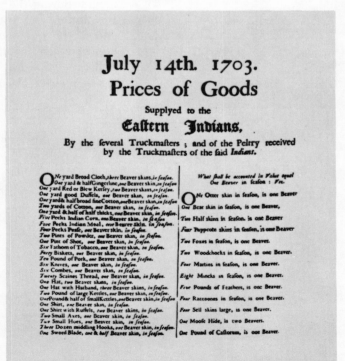

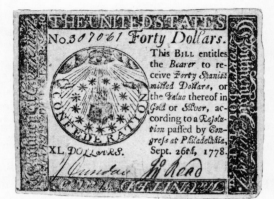

The Continental Congress issued paper money during the Revolution, but by the end of the war one hundred Continental dollars were worth only a single silver Spanish dollar.

on metal coins, preferably silver. In the War of 1812 the Treasury issued notes, but these were promises to pay which were treated more like present-day bonds than money. State banks issued bank notes that circulated widely and served as money, but the banks could and did fail, leaving their paper currency as worthless souvenirs.

In 1861—in the midst of another war—paper money made its return. Congress printed greenbacks, so called because one side was printed in green. These were not backed by gold or silver. Nonetheless, in 1862 Congress passed a law stating they were legal tender, that is, they had to be accepted by any creditor in payment of a debt. The Confederacy also issued paper currency, some of it backed by the South's staple crop, cotton. The value of both currencies, Federal and Confederate, fluctuated widely in European markets as the war seesawed back and forth; with the Union victory, the millions of Confederate bills became worthless. The Federal greenbacks did not immediately become highly valued but Congress passed legislation establishing a national banking system to support the national currency. Finally, fourteen years after the war, Congress passed a law stating that the bills could be redeemed for gold. But by this time both the greenbacks and the government had won public confidence. There was no rush to the Treasury for gold. Sound paper money—similar to the kind we know today —had been established.

There have been other chapters in the history of modern money, and perhaps one of the blackest was that

The Confederacy circulated paper currency; with the Union victory, the bills became worthless.

experienced by Germany during and after its defeat in World War I. At the start of the war Germany had two billion marks in circulation; at the end it had five hundred quintillion (500,000,000,000,000,000,000). In 1923 it took one trillion paper marks to buy what a single prewar mark had bought, that is, something worth about twenty-four cents. Toward the end of 1923 German em-

A clay two mark piece, issued as "necessity money" during the German inflation after World War I.

ployers paid their workers daily so that they could roll a wheelbarrow load of notes around to buy groceries. At the end of the year prices rose so fast new paper money lost half its value in an hour.

There is a story told about a Russian refugee who fled the Bolshevik revolution with little more than two pieces of the family jewels. She lived comfortably in Berlin during the inflation by pawning first one jewel and then the other. She borrowed money on the first and when it was used up she pawned the second—getting enough money to redeem the first, plus an additional sum to pay the rent and buy groceries. When that was gone, the first jewel would go into hock again, this time worth more than ever in terms of the deteriorating currency, so that the second jewel could be redeemed and the whole process started again. The spiral of inflation had to come to an end sometime, and in 1924 the postwar German government had to repudiate all previous currency and introduce a new mark—this one in severely limited quantities so that it would command respect. Once more, it had been shown that a government that relies solely on the printing press, and not on sound fiscal policies, creates chaos and hardship for most of its citizens.

2 / MONEY, GOOD OR BAD

WHAT MAKES SOME money as worthless as a 1920 German mark and other money as sound as a dollar? Is the dollar really sound? Can we be sure it will stay that way? These are some of the questions that economists puzzle over and argue about. The fact of the matter is that money and its place in modern life is full of mysteries that have only recently been better understood.

In today's world you cannot tell good money from bad by biting it or weighing it or studying it to see if Henry VIII's copper nose is showing through. It's even more difficult to detect counterfeit paper money because of the expert up-to-date photoengraving techniques used by counterfeiters. What's more, a good deal of the money that changes hands in the American economy—representing nine-tenths of all transactions—is in a form we don't commonly think of as money at all. It is not quarters and dimes, dollar bills or fives, tens, twenties. It consists of a few words and numbers written or typed on a piece of paper called a check. A check is a call on "money in the bank"—an order to the banker to pay the money in one person's account to another person. Checking accounts are described as demand deposits, ready to be paid out on command. In today's world, they constitute the most common form of money there is.

Since there have been so many changes in the kinds and forms of money during man's history, it might be a good idea to find out just what money is—what it is that the pieces of eight have in common with greenbacks and Federal Reserve notes.

There is a saying, "Money is as money does." Or as a British economist, R. G. Hawtrey, has put it: "Money is one of those concepts which, like a teaspoon or an umbrella, but unlike an earthquake or a buttercup, are definable primarily by the use or purpose which they serve." In other words, you can't tell if something is actually money by looking at it; you have to know if it functions as money.

Economists have decided that there are three, or possibly four, things that money should do to be true money. First, it should function as a medium of exchange; that is, it should serve as a convenient way to exchange a week's work for food and rent, clothes, payments on a car, and so forth. Second, money should function as "units of account." This simply means that we measure the worth of many things in terms of money—a quart of milk, an automobile, a plumber's charge for an hour of labor, or a doctor's housecall, all have their price tags. Third, money should be a "liquid asset"; that is, something you can carry in your pocket and, within an instant, turn into something else, such as a meal in a restaurant, a ticket to Hawaii, a new hat. Fourth, some economists had described money as a "store of value," something that can be put in a strongbox now and spent ten years hence to buy a pair of shoes or a cabin in the country. Today we are less likely to keep money in our possession than we are to put it in savings accounts in the bank, or in government bonds or some other form of investment. This is sometimes called "near money," since it is not immediately available.

It is important to note that these functions are all closely related. We use money as a means of measuring the value of goods and the worth of an hour of labor because it can be exchanged for them. Its functions as a liquid asset or a store of value again go back to its use as a medium of exchange. And its acceptability as a medium of exchange depends in part on its other qualities. Money would be less readily accepted as a medium of exchange if we didn't know it was a liquid asset—spendable at any time. And we wouldn't save it if we didn't think it would be spendable some time in the future.

These functions of money are tests to tell us if something is in fact money. If a paper bill or a string of shells or something else—cigarettes, for instance—meet these tests, then we can properly call it money. Cigarettes did serve as money in prisoner-of-war camps during World War II, and they continued to serve in defeated Germany for a short while after the war because the Germans were shy of any renewal of the inflation of World War I.

While economists agree that many things can serve as money, they also make an important distinction between wealth and money. Money can be used to measure wealth —but wealth, real wealth, the economists say, consists of things that are valuable for themselves. Diamonds, valued paintings, land, buildings, factories, oil wells, mines, steel mills, power plants, things that can be used to make something desirable—these represent wealth. A millionaire, for instance, is not likely to have a million dollars in cash. We call him a millionaire because he owns things that are worth a million dollars—and the things may consist of land, apartment buildings, a fleet of taxicabs, a thriving restaurant or two, or certificates called stocks which represent the ownership of business enterprises. Modern millionaires put their money to work.

What money is, what it is not, and what it does are all fairly easy to understand. Why it does its job as money is not always so simple.

The key to "why" anything serves as money seems to lie in its acceptability. In the days of primitive man, it became a practice to trade tools and tools became acceptable as a medium of exchange. Then precious metals, then coins began to change hands among people who were reasonably sure that other people would accept them. We can guess that there were some people who wouldn't have anything to do with various new-fangled forms of money, people who preferred to barter, swapping their

The vaultlike U.S. Bullion Depository at Fort Knox, Kentucky.

labor or their belongings directly for the things they needed. But the first coins must have become good sound money as more and more people saw that they could be readily exchanged for desired goods, saw that they were both convenient and safe.

Paper money had to withstand the same test of acceptability, and as its history shows, there have been many times when paper money has not been accepted readily. And it's quite reasonable to predict that there will be other times when various paper currencies will be regarded as dubious in value because people come to distrust them because they fear they won't be accepted by others.

How about our own paper currency? Can it always be trusted? It costs the United States Bureau of Engraving and Printing less than a cent to produce a dollar bill, or even a twenty dollar bill. What makes each bill worth the amount printed on its corners?

Ask this question of some of your friends and you'll get various answers: Because the government stands behind it. Because Congress has passed laws making it legal tender, acceptable for the payment of debts. Because of all the gold in Fort Knox.

Good answers—all of them, and taken together they sum up the situation. The action of the government has a great deal to do with the soundness of our money. Such things as the national debt, our banking system, our taxes, the health of our economy and the efficiency of law enforcement officers in tracking down counterfeiters all have a part in the intertangled, often mysterious, often bewildering question of money.

Our stock of gold in Fort Knox is important, as well, for the dollar in today's world is constantly being compared with the British pound, the Soviet ruble, the German mark, Swiss and French francs, and scores of other currencies. And it is here that gold comes in, for gold is the one form of international money that is almost universally recognized.

There are people who believe our money should be tied more firmly to gold than it is at present: that we need a full-fledged return to the gold standard. There are others who say we are mad to worry about gold at all, that it is one of the idiocies of our civilization that men dig up gold in one hole in the ground in places like South Africa and Siberia only to have it buried again at Fort Knox or underneath the Federal Reserve Bank on Liberty Street in downtown New York City.

Yet gold has been a highly respected kind of money for centuries. It is not easy to argue it out of existence and perhaps not desirable. Adolf Hitler once poured scorn on the use of gold as money; he said the world's bankers would never find enough cavities so that dentists could use up their useless hoards. But his Nazis dug gold fillings out of the teeth of hapless concentration camp victims and looted the treasuries of the nations they overran as quickly as they could in order to get their hands on the bullion stores. Marx and Lenin ridiculed the use of gold as money, yet the Soviet Union mines some of the world's most extensive gold deposits with considerable diligence, guarding figures of production as a state secret. The reason is simple enough: gold can buy things in world markets, when paper rubles by themselves cannot. This was very clearly demonstrated in 1963 when the Soviet Union bought shiploads of grain from Canada and the United States and paid for them by selling unusually large quantities of gold for the kind of currency—dollars —acceptable to the grain dealers.

The relationship between the dollar and gold is not always clearly understood. It is common to recall that we "went off the gold standard" in 1933; we haven't done anything to go back on the gold standard since then; and yet our money does have a direct and vital connection to gold. We did not, in fact, part company with the gold standard in 1933. What happened was that the government stopped issuing gold coins and began issuing gold certificates only to Federal Reserve banks, not to the public. It became an offense to hoard gold. At the same time, the dollar was devalued, that is, it became worth less in terms of gold than before. It was then that the value of the dollar was fixed at 1/35 of a fine ounce of gold; or to put it another way, the price of gold was fixed at $35 an ounce, where it has stayed ever since. This price has become a fixed part of our monetary policy—one that Presidents Eisenhower, Kennedy, and Johnson have been at pains to reaffirm and pledge themselves to defend. Thus, the Treasury is committed to exchange gold for dollars, or dollars for gold, at this ratio on world money markets. (But not with its own citizens at home who may not legally hoard gold.) This basic relationship between the dollar and gold is what puts us on what today passes for the gold standard—sometimes called the "gold exchange standard." The Treasury describes it either as a "gold bullion standard" or a "modified gold standard."

Our money, then, has a definite link with gold, the traditional international money. But this alone does not explain or set the limits of government action to regulate the value of the dollar. A great many other things—including the Treasury, our banking system, monetary controls, interest rates—go into this.

3 / GUARDING OUR MONEY

THE CONSTITUTION SAYS: "The Congress shall have power to coin money, regulate the value thereof, and of foreign coin . . . to provide for the punishment of counterfeiting the securities and common coin of the United States." Since these few lines of authority went into our basic law, the nation's legislators, presidents, secretaries of treasury, and a host of others have devoted much time and effort to the problem of keeping our money sound. It is still one of the biggest worries in the world, as witness constant controversies about the national debt, taxes, the loss of gold, and the cost of living.

One aspect of this concern is delegated to a corner of the United States Treasury where the Secret Service has its headquarters. This is the problem of making counterfeiting so unprofitable that it does not affect the value of our money. The Secret Service takes this job seriously, tracking down phoney bills and their draftsmen, lead nickels and their coiners. They do their work inside and outside of the United States with such diligence that other officials, and the public at large, rarely have to think twice about it. Counterfeiting doesn't pay.

Still some people seem to want to learn this the hard way. They think they can get rich quick by breaking the monopoly for printing currency alloted to the Bureau of Engraving and Printing or for clicking out new coins assigned to the Mint. They have visions of huge piles of nice new money, all their own, fresh and homemade. They do not, however, keep and cherish their creations when they come from the press or coin machine. Counterfeiters are always eager to exchange their own, brand new stuff for beaten and frayed bills or old and battered coinage. Genuine money fascinates them, too. A phoney buck is something to be got rid of fast, something to palm off on someone else in favor of the real, unchallengable article from the Treasury. For the counterfeiter, possession of his own handiwork is risky, and an invitation to a prison term. "Queer" money, "curly," gives the underworld an uneasy feeling. It recalls the story of the eighteenth-century French thief who stole a packet of bills one night and returned them the next, leaving a note: "These are counterfeit. Guard yourself. There are rogues about."

Rogues continue to make the attempt. They use many techniques. Some years back, one of them threw a twenty-dollar bill down on bar and would have walked off with his change but for a small thing. The bartender got the bill wet and noticed that the color ran, something he knew that never happens to real bills. He said he had to get change and called the police. When they quizzed the culprit, they found he had painstakingly drawn the bill line by line with pen and ink, and done a presentable, deceptive job of it. He is known with wonderment in Secret Service annals as "Jim the Penman."

Until a few years ago, most currency counterfeiters used to be skilled engravers, and the T-men kept files on known practitioners with a weakness for larceny. When a new outbreak of creative printing came along, they checked out their list. The list was usually relatively short, for engraving is a highly trained occupation, with, of course, many, many honest workers for every dishonest one. Today the Secret Service still has this short list for investigating engraved forgeries but it also has to contend with many more attempts being made with the help of the newest techniques of photoengraving. These techniques—increasingly used to produce better pictures in books and magazines, on posters and packages—make it relatively easy to turn out a printing plate that will do a fair job of reproducing a bill, if one doesn't look too closely.

In a recent annual report on the problem, Secret Service Chief James R. Rowley said that present-day counterfeiters sometimes gain access to expensive modern printing plant equipment of a legitimate enterprise, make their plates, turn out bogus money, destroy the plates, and go on their way. Sometimes these are plant employees who use the equipment after normal working hours without the knowledge or consent of their employers. In one case,

The U.S. Treasury Department Building in Washington, D.C.

a counterfeiter rented machinery, ran off his homemade bills, and returned the equipment before leaving town. In the fiscal year 1962–63, Mr. Rowley reported that his agents had seized $2,845,823 in phoney money before it could be passed. Another $548,400 in fake money went into circulation and represented a loss to the public— because when an innocent recipient finds himself with a bogus bill, he bears the loss. Six hundred and sixty-two persons were arrested during the year for counterfeiting. Still it was a better year for honest money than the year before. In 1962, the Secret Service seized $3,567,020 of unpassed counterfeit money, the public was stuck for $567,896, and 737 persons were pinched by the T-men.

Fortunately bills produced with a camera never come

up to the standards of sharpness and distinctiveness of the work turned out by the Bureau of Engraving in the shadow of the Washington Monument. The skilled draftsmen of the Treasury work with soft steel plates and very hard tools. Each line they etch in the metal varies in length, width, and depth. It takes one of these artists a month to make one of the portraits that appear on a bill and one wrong stroke can ruin it. Parts of the bill are etched with a geometric lathe which cuts complicated patterns that can be duplicated only when the lathe settings are known. The designs of our bills have offended many people who think they are cluttered and inartistic. Part of the clutter is specifically designed to foil artistic forgers, as well as larcenous cameramen.

The Treasury urges Americans to take a closer look at their money in order to appreciate the finer points of this engraving, and in order to be able to tell when someone is trying to palm off a phoney note. Look at the portrait of George Washington on a one dollar bill, Abraham Lincoln on a five, Alexander Hamilton on a ten. If you want to carry your research further—and if you are rich enough—you can also examine the portrait of Benjamin Franklin on a $100 bill or, better yet, Salmon P. Chase on the $10,000 Federal Reserve Note. On a genuine bill the eyes are sharp and lifelike, the shading of the face gives a good likeness of natural flesh tones, the lines that show the folds of the clothing are sharp and clear, the cross-hatching of the dark background shows distinct lines. On a bogus photoengraving none of these things are true. Instead the eyes are blurred; the flesh tones are smudged, the folds of the cloth are indistinct and the background tends to be a muddy black. Another thing to look for is the blue or green seal on the portrait side. On good bills, the points on this seal are always sharp, uniform, and distinct. On phonies they are usually uneven and broken off. Serial numbers on good currency are also sharp and evenly spaced whereas counterfeit money often has poorly printed, badly spaced numbers.

The Treasury takes a lot of trouble with other features of our paper money. The green ink is made from a secret formula and the Treasury uses four million pounds a year. The paper contains blue and red cotton threads just barely detectable in new bills, usually not at all in old ones. It is produced in a single factory in Massachusetts under close security. The paper is tough; it can be folded two thousand times at the same place without tearing. Even so the average dollar bill lasts a year and a half or less; bigger denominations last longer for the simple reason that they are exchanged less frequently. The Bureau of Engraving and Printing has to print its most valuable piece of currency only rarely. This is the $100,000 gold certificate bearing a picture of Woodrow Wilson. Gold certificates are used by the Federal Reserve banks to settle their own accounts; they are not paid out by the banks and they do not appear in circulation. Our normal paper money comes in three kinds—silver certificates, United States notes, and Federal Reserve notes. All our one dollar bills used to be silver certificates and there are also five dollar silver certificates. They carry inscriptions stating that "there is on deposit in the Treasury of the United States of America one dollar in silver payable to the bearer on demand." Now, however, silver certificates are on the way out as our principal form of low denomination bills. They are giving way to Federal Reserve notes. This is the result of the "demonetization" of silver progressively approved by Congress in recent years. The basic reason is that silver, a metal increasingly useful in electronics, photography, and the space age has been rising in price and has become too expensive to serve in its old capacity in our money system.

The second form of paper money, United States notes, has been issued in two and five dollar denominations. In 1966 the Treasury decided to stop issuing two dollar bills "because of a lack of public demand." Such bills go back a long way—they were first printed in this denomination in 1776—but they came to be regarded either as bad luck or an awkward currency form. So much so that they lasted three to four times longer than one and five dollar bills, with many of them sitting in bank vaults, unwanted by the public.

Far more common now than either silver certificates or United States notes are Federal Reserve notes. These used to come in fives, tens, twenties, and upward to $10,000. Since the shift away from silver, they are also being issued in one dollar bills. Older Federal Reserve notes carry the guarantee that they may be taken to the Treasury or any Federal Reserve bank and redeemed in "lawful money."

This has puzzled some people, because presumably it means the bankers can hand back a like amount of the same kind of notes, since they are, indeed, lawful money. This statement has been replaced on new one dollar bills with the following statement, "This note is legal tender for all debts, public and private."

The Treasury guards all parts of the printing, issuing, handling, and even destruction of our currency with scrupulous care. It churns out dollar bills on high-speed rotary presses using a dry intaglio press. In intaglio printing the ink is *inside* the grooves on the plate, not on the flat surfaces as in ordinary letterpress printing; where groove meets paper, a line of ink is left behind. Separate processes put seals and numbers on the notes. Cutting the paper, counting, inspecting, and rechecking are carried out under exacting controls to prevent error or hanky-panky. Still, mistakes can creep in. There's a Washington postman who carries around an authentic dollar bill with George Washington staring out on both sides. It may be valuable—newspaper accounts say he refused on offer of $300 for it. The Bureau of Engraving regrets such honest errors, pointing out that twelve separate inspections are supposed to eliminate them. The premium value collectors put in such monetary freaks leaves the Treasury cold and unmoved. It says the two-headed bill is worth exactly one dollar.

As for larceny, a Bureau of Engraving handyman a few years back managed to smuggle two packages containing 8,000 tightly wrapped twenties—$160,000—out

The U.S. Mint in Denver, Colorado, can produce as many as twelve million coins a day.

of the Bureau's creaky building near Washington's Tidal Basin. But he didn't get very far; he had to give them all back and answer to the law as well. Treasury officials say that new money, with serial numbers freshly recorded, is easy to trace. They try to make it difficult to filch old money, too. Worn silver certificates and U.S. notes—ones, twos, and fives—are burned at Federal Reserve banks and Treasury branches throughout the country by carefully prescribed procedures and by special officials. Federal Reserve notes are collected at the same points, stamped full of holes and cut in half lengthwise. One half is shipped to the Treasury in Washington one day and the other half on another, ending up in ashes in an incinerator. Strange precautions, until you recall that most of the $7,250,000 stolen from a British mail car by a gang of criminal commandos in the Great Train Robbery of 1963 consisted of old English bank notes going to London whole for retirement from circulation and destruction.

The Bureau of the Mint takes the same care with coins that Engraving does with currency. It has mechanized mints in Denver and Philadelphia that can produce as many as twelve million coins a day. Recently two and a half billion coins were struck in one year. The Mint responds to the needs and whims of the country. A new cigarette tax means an extra shipment of pennies. Silver dollars go West. Half dollars are popular in Boston. Just before Christmas, when everyone is spending, the Mint tries to furnish the Federal Reserve system with more coins than usual. Its new coins go out, shiny and sharp, with reeded edges to prevent coin trimmers from sweating a little metal off each piece. Old coins come back smooth and thin and are melted down with the same kind of precautions that goes with the incineration of old bank notes.

T-men track down bogus coin makers just as they do paper currency counterfeiters. In 1955 they worried about a flood of 1944 Jefferson nickels. It was a fairly good reproduction but it had a flaw in the *r* in *E Pluribus Unum* and no *P* for the Philadelphia mint. Who would want to counterfeit a nickel? Was there any profit in it? They followed a few clues, found some machinery dumped in a river and finally caught up with an engineer who had been able to earn as much as $12,000 a year at honest jobs. He had spent $25,000 of his own money assembling a high-pressure stamping machine, a blast furnace, and a supply of cupronickel of the same chemical analysis as that used in genuine coins. He had been depositing $60 at a time in counterfeit nickels in Philadelphia banks but not for very long. He was prosecuted and sentenced to a three-year prison term and a $5,000 fine—and a substantial net loss on the whole transaction.

Counterfeiters with such an inept sense of profit and loss are almost laughable, but not to the nation's lawmakers and keepers. The late Supreme Court justice, Robert H. Jackson, once summed up the matter in this fashion:

Counterfeiting is an offense never committed by accident, nor by ignorance, nor in heat of passion, nor in extremity of poverty. It is a crime expertly designed by one who possesses technical skill and lays out substantial sums for equipment. It is a crime not excused by the fact that "everyone is doing it." Counterfeiters are few and are not amateur criminals. It is not a crime of courage. It is a sneaking offense, and it cheats small tradesmen and unsuspecting people who have not the skill or experience to detect the imitation.

Throughout the world governments take a similar dim view when their money is being tampered with. A French finance minister recently set the police on the trail of a counterfeiter of one franc coins—worth about twenty cents—because his work was a "hemorrhage" on the national treasury. The British counterfeited Continental dollars systematically in the Revolutionary War as a means of weakening the young republic. In the 1920's a Portuguese swindler, by means of impersonations and forged letters, managed to get trunkloads of Portuguese currency delivered to him by the British company that furnished the Lisbon government with its official and legitimate supply. When the fraud was discovered, it produced a national crisis. The Nazis in World War II established what is probably the most elaborate counterfeiting plot of all time. They set up shop in a concentration camp, assembled a team of skilled inmates from their millions of prisoners, promised them survival and favorable treatment, and went to work forging English five pound notes. "Operation Bernhard," as it was called, eventually printed millions of dollars worth of bogus British currency. Large amounts of these "fivers" circulated on the European continent and elsewhere—the frugal, unscrupulous Nazis even used them to pay their spies—but very few were accepted by the Bank of England. As soon as the first trickle was discovered, the Bank simply withdrew all five pound notes from circulation and relied on untainted one pound notes. Counterfeiting on an international scale and as an act of war called for stern defensive measures—another indication that safeguards for a nation's money are a part of national security.

4 / MR. HAMILTON'S HANDIWORK

WARDING OFF COUNTERFEITERS is only part of the task of keeping our money sound—and some officials and economic experts think it is the easier part. At least the law is clear—counterfeiters are "the bad guys"; the T-men are the "good guys" who track them down. But the business that comes under the constitutional provision that Congress "shall have the power . . . to regulate the value" of our money has to be guided by far less certain rules of what is right and wrong. The value of our money is directly related to government economic policy, which in turn is related to the state of our economy and, more and more in modern times, to the state of the world. Thus, American money managers are continually assaulted by critics who say what is wrong with our money is that our national debt is too big, or our interest rates are too high, or our interest rates are too low. Congress and the two government agencies which have the most to do with our money—the Treasury and the Federal Reserve Board—are never without someone to give them free advice. Unfortunately it is rare when all their advisers agree on any one line of action; often there are two, three, or perhaps four schools of thought pulling in different directions.

The Treasury, of course, is the agency that has the most direct dealings with money. It prints and coins it, collects it in taxes, and pays it out for space capsules, tons of paper, battleships, salaries, loans to farmers, old-age pensions. It is the Treasury's worry when federal income doesn't keep up with outgo, a disturbing but fairly common occurrence. It is a worry of long standing. The Continental Congress during the Revolution and afterward had a succession of committees, joint treasurers, and superintendents of finance to fret over its debts, its depreciating currency, counterfeiting problems, and the like. With the ratification of the Constitution, the new Congress quickly provided for a Secretary of the Treasury. He and his department were charged with collecting and managing federal government revenue, estimating and reporting on public expenditures, keeping the government's accounts, and performing other chores, not all of them fiscal. President Washington chose as the first Secretary a young man of thirty-two, Alexander Hamilton, who had previously served him as his aide-de-camp. After all these years Hamilton's presence is still very much felt around the Treasury. His statue stands at the south steps of the big colonnaded Treasury Building just east of the White House. His portrait has a prominent place within the high-ceilinged building. And still another portrait is on our ten dollar bill.

The reasons for all these honors are simple enough. Hamilton was Mr. Fiscal Integrity himself. Of modest

Hamilton helped set up the Bank of New York, an institution noted for its financial orthodoxy—and for its survival through all of America's financial turbulence up to the present.

origins, he had married into one of the richest families in
New York and, at the age of twenty-eight, helped set up
the Bank of New York, an institution noted for its financial
orthodoxy—and for its survival through all of America's
financial turbulence up to the present. Hamilton sat in
the Constitutional Convention and wrote more than half
the *Federalist Essays* urging the adoption of the Constitution. He wanted a strong national government, a strong
Treasury, a national bank, and uniform national taxation.
Without these things, he argued that the power of money
in the new Republic would be divisive, the source of
quarrels and conflict. "For it is an observation, as true
as it is trite," he wrote, "that there is nothing men differ
so readily about as the payment of money." And he offered
a banker's shudder over the recent Shays Rebellion in
Massachusetts; it was an outbreak of civil war, he said,
that would not have happened if Shays had not been
"such a *desperate debtor*." The italics for emphasis were
his.

When he became secretary, Hamilton fought for the
recognition of the war debts of the Confederation, both
those owed to foreign governments and to its own citizens.
This delighted speculators who had bought up debt certificates cheaply when it appeared that the government
would not honor them. But it also meant the new Republic
began with an excellent credit rating. Another Hamilton
achievement was the creation of a Bank of the United
States—an institution that had many ups and downs in
the years ahead but served as something of a forerunner

to our present national banking system. Still another Hamilton accomplishment: a "Report on the Establishment of a Mint." This became the basis for the Coinage Act of 1792, a law that established the dollar as the unit of American currency based on the decimal system.

Hamilton was also instrumental in establishing the United States Coast Guard; he wanted it in order to stamp out smuggling because the young government drew most of its revenue from custom duties. Today—some fifty secretaries later—this is no longer the case. The Treasury's Bureau of Internal Revenue collects more than half the federal government's intake from the sixty million people who file income tax returns every year. Another big slice comes from the business firms that pay corporate income taxes. Only about 1 per cent comes from customs.

The national debt about which Hamilton was concerned amounted to a few million dollars, a paltry sum compared with the present-day total of about 335 billion dollars. The size of this debt is something the Secretary of the Treasury and his aides can do little about. The Congress appropriates the money that is spent and passes the tax laws that bring in the revenue. The Bureau of the Budget, an independent office outside the Treasury, helps the President prepare his annual budget message on which Congress acts. All the government's agencies run up the bills which the Treasury pays with something like four hundred million checks a year. These green IBM cards are authorized by the Treasurer of the United States—not to be confused with the Secretary—and

President Washington chose Alexander Hamilton to be the first Secretary of the Treasury.

signed by her aides. (Recent Treasurers have been women.)

Every year congressmen talk about how high the national debt is. It isn't hard to see how it got that way—and where the money is still going. World War II sent the national debt soaring from 50 billion dollars to more than 250 billion. The Korean War sent it up another step toward the 300 billion dollar level. About half of the more than 100 billion dollars that the Treasury currently collects each year is spent by the Defense Department for the rockets, Polaris submarines, and atomic devices that provide the necessary but costly defense of our freedom.

The Treasury does more than record the debts. It also has to find places to borrow the money—and keep it borrowed. It does this by selling bonds and, when they are redeemed, selling more bonds. This is what the experts call "managing the national debt."

The Treasury, like any other borrower, is able to get people to lend it money because the lenders are certain the money will be returned. Here, Hamilton's policy, and the policies of other secretaries who have followed him, have paid off; by honoring its debts consistently, the United States government has been able to maintain a very good reputation as a credit risk. Even so, when people lend it money, they want something more than assurance of its return. They want payment for the use of their money—and this payment, of course, is interest.

The Treasury's best known bargain for individual lenders is what used to be known as a Defense War Bond, dating back to its origin in World War II. Now they are simply called Savings Bonds. Buy one for $75 and receive $100 in seven years and nine months. This represents an interest rate of 4.15 per cent. The smallest denomination is the $25 bond which costs $18.75. One major advantage of these bonds is that they can be cashed in at any time at the cost price plus, for as they approach maturity, there is an increasing amount of accrued interest.

U.S. Savings Bonds are a deservedly tempting and popular offer to many Americans. They are nice to tuck in Christmas stockings. Teenagers stack them up toward college. Thrifty people take them in place of part of their regular paycheck under payroll deduction systems—a particularly effective way of saving. Would-be homeowners accumulate them toward a down payment on a house. And retired persons can cash them in to supplement their other retirement income.

The Treasury has about $50 billion in Savings Bonds outstanding, representing a little less than one-sixth of the national debt. Its other bonds fall into far fewer hands, come in larger denominations ($1,000 a bond), may be long or short term and pay varying rates of interest, sometimes less, sometimes more than Savings Bonds. Banks, corporations, and wealthy individuals buy these bonds. Like the bonds of the States and various public agencies and those of business firms, these bonds are promises to pay a certain amount of money at a certain date. There is no obligation to cash them in at any fixed figure before the maturity date. Of course, such a promise-to-pay by the United States government is always worth something substantial, and there is a market for them—people willing to buy them. But their value will fluctuate according to such factors as current interest rates or whether money available for lending is "easy" or "tight." Investors have found that it is possible to buy a Treasury bond for $1,000 and discover, a year or so later, that it can be sold on the market for only $900.

It's also possible (as I write this) to buy bonds for $875, that will be redeemed for $1,000 twenty years hence, bonds which pay interest of 3¼ per cent in the meantime. A year or so from now, bargains like this may have disappeared. The vagaries of the government bond market are not something everyone can follow. But Treasury men, particularly those in the Bureau of the Public Debt, follow it very closely. They have to pay out almost nine and a half billion dollars in interest on the national debt every year. When they can redeem a few billion dollars worth of 4 per cent bonds and replace them with 3½ per cent bonds the savings are apt to make even a millionaire's head swim. A .5 per cent reduction in interest on 10 billion dollars is worth 50 million dollars a year. Even so, the Treasury can't consider interest rates all important; soundness of the dollar, the nation's general economic and monetary health, must come first.

5 / THE FEDERAL RESERVE

IF YOU FOLLOW money in action today, you inevitably come to a bank. If you are interested in the soundness of the dollar, or the state of the economy, you must explore the complex but fascinating world of banking. Banks are places where a great deal of our money is deposited—and rather astonishing things can happen to it while it is there. For instance, it can stay right in the bank, while we are busy spending it. We'll see how later in this chapter. What's more, the experts will tell you that banks can and do *create* money. It's the banking system, they say, that has the most to do with how much money is in circulation, how the quantity of money necessary to do the nation's business expands and contracts, grows bigger, then smaller. To the ordinary person, the non-banker, this sounds like a form of magic too good to be true. If bankers can create money, why are the rest of us working so hard for it? What kind of magic does a banker use to conjure up money where none existed before?

Obviously a bank is more than a place to keep one's money for safety's sake. Banks began their life providing safety. Merchants in London, for instance, began leaving their gold and coins with city goldsmiths, rather than have them stored in the Tower of London where a greedy King might grab them. The goldsmiths gave receipts which entitled the person who held them to recover the gold. Then someone found that it was much easier to give a gold receipt to a person to whom he owed money than it was to take the receipt to the smith, collect the heavy metal, and hand that over instead. The receipts began to circulate as money—the first bank notes. The next step came when the goldsmith-bankers decided that they could lend out such bank-note receipts even when they did not have sufficient gold to back up every one of their pieces of paper. This was when they began to create money in the sense that bankers talk about. Their new promises to provide gold were now backed by someone else's promises to repay the loan. The bankers took such a step because they knew from experience that all the holders of their receipts were not very likely to come and ask that the receipts be redeemed for precious metal at the same time. The bankers thus had a reserve of gold— but a reserve that did not cover their total obligations. These total obligations were now backed partly by the gold on deposit and partly by the promises to repay that the debtors had given. When the bankers' reserves became low in relation to their outstanding paper notes, they called upon their debtors to make repayment, or they were less free with making new loans, or they charged a higher rate of interest on their loans—or a combination of all three. The bankers, then, had something to say about how big the money supply was—how it increased or contracted.

This is still the classic pattern of bank-created money. Over the years, there has been many a new variation, but the fundamental principle is still the same. The changes mostly have to do with preventing the things that can go wrong with the system.

And things can go wrong. Suppose, for instance, Thomas Woolsack, London merchant, had some gold coins on deposit with Foolhardy Brothers, Cosset Lane bankers. One day, let us imagine, Woolsack heard a story in a coffee house that the Foolhardy Brothers had been making extensive loans to a group of tea importers who were awaiting a big shipment from India. The merchants had already used a good part of the Foolhardy gold coin reserves to build ships, buy tea, and so forth. The shipment was crucial, in fact, to both the tea merchants who were committed to repay these loans and to the bank that financed them. The story that Thomas Woolsack heard was that the incoming ship with all that tea aboard had gone down in a fierce storm in the Atlantic within sight of England. Woolsack hurried down to Cosset Lane to draw his money out of the Foolhardy Brothers bank, and he found a long line of unhappy depositors. It was a run on the bank. It was soon apparent that the Foolhardy Brothers and their bank were broke—and there was nothing much that most of the depositors could do. The money just wasn't there.

The history of banking has had many stories of this kind—failures and scandals both individual and collective. Fortunately they have usually been followed by investigation and reform which have produced newer, better, and stronger banks. And this has been because banks, and the many varied financial institutions like them, are simply such useful things that people haven't been able to get along without them.

American banking has had as many ups and downs as those in other countries. Hamilton's Bank of the United States had its enemies among Jefferson's Whigs who thought that a big national institution favored the wealthy merchants of New York and New England rather than southern farmers and the frontiersmen. The bank's charter was allowed to run out in 1811. It was set up again in 1817, but Andrew Jackson, like Jefferson, despised it, called it "a monster" and "hydra of corruption." It finally expired after the Panic of 1837. During this period, Congress left a wide open field for state-chartered banks that had the right to issue bank notes. Some of these soon became known as "wildcat banks"—that is, their offices were located in wildcat infested woods, making it difficult for someone who had accepted one of their notes to find the proper business premises where it presumably could be exchanged for gold or silver. Another term used was

Checks began to be used in the mid-nineteenth century. This one is signed by Jefferson Davis.

"saddlebag banks"—the bankers were always on the move. During the chaos that existed up to 1865 there were as many as seven thousand different kinds of paper bank notes circulating in the United States.

Despite the confusion, American banks began growing up during the period before and after the Civil War. Checks began to be used for business transactions in the 1850's. These useful pieces of paper might be written against one bank and deposited in another. They had to be exchanged promptly. Bank messengers used to race back and forth in cities like New York, Philadelphia, and Boston, sometimes colliding with each other as they carried money and checks back and forth. Then Boston and New York set up clearing houses, central points where all the banks in a city could exchange payments. During the Civil War a system of nationally chartered banks grew up. They had the right to issue bank notes provided they had

The Panic of 1837,

as depicted in a satiric cartoon of the period.

reserves in federal government bonds (90 per cent) and cash reserves of 15 to 25 per cent of their total notes and deposits.

The times were changing; a nation was growing. Railroads were stretching across the country, Andrew Carnegie was building steel mills in Pittsburgh, immigrants were streaming through New York to work on farms and in factories. There were more and more banks, with more depositors and more things to lend money for. The growth of bigger industry meant greater use of the stock market. Big companies were not owned by one man or one family but by scores and hundreds of individuals who held, as a token of their ownership, company shares. And these shares were to be sold and bought on the stock exchanges. The more complicated the transactions became, the more banks were used—and the more different kinds of banks and related institutions came into being. At the same time, the government played a considerably smaller role in the economy than it now does. The need for government intervention wasn't apparent and there were few people who wanted the government in business for its own sake; that was not the American way.

Still, as the nineteenth century ended and the twentieth began, there were times when everything did not seem sound, healthy or fair in the business world. Powerful figures arose who would try to "corner the market" on wheat and drive the price up, something that made bread dearer in the home of the average man. Then there were "trusts" that did the same thing for steel and for the oil

America was using for light and heat. Some of the news-papers said there was even a "money trust" presided over by one of the most powerful of all figures in the business world, J. P. Morgan. This flashing-eyed, black-coated sober man, with a heavy gold chain at his vest, was not the richest of the country's millionaires but he was un-doubtedly the most influential, a true financier. Mr. Doo-ley, Finley Peter Dunne's fictional Irish saloon keeper, described him as ordering one of his office boys to take some small change out of the till to buy Europe and reorganize it on a paying basis. In London, where Morgan was a frequent visitor and transactor of business, peddlers offered for a penny a "license to stay on Earth" jokingly said to be signed "J. Pierpont Morgan."

The House of Morgan was involved in many enterprises, including steel and railroads, but it was most deeply in-volved in banking and it was inevitably caught up in any banking crisis. In 1907 America had a banking crisis —one of the successions of boom and bust that seemed to accompany modern industrialization. The future would look bright and rosy one year and people would invest their money freely in new enterprises, certain that there were huge profits to be gained. Banks would lend money freely—and the more borrowed money there was the more speculation would follow. Then the mood would change for one reason or another and people would begin to ask whether the future was really so promising, whether stock prices were not really too high for the real earning capacity of the businesses they represented. Once the questioning process began, people began to try to convert things they owned into cash. And if there wasn't enough cash there would be trouble.

In October 1907 several New York banks had to appeal for help from the New York Clearing House when the public learned that their officers had lost a large sum of money in a copper company stock venture. Rumors began flying, particularly about one type of bank, the trust company, that had been allowed to operate almost like national banks but without the same strict regulations. One of these was the Knickerbocker Trust Company, an imposing looking organization located on New York's Fifth Avenue opposite the old Waldorf-Astoria Hotel in the midst of one of the city's most prosperous and modern neighborhoods. On October 22 the thing that had been feared—a run on the bank—took place. And by 2 P.M. the Knickerbocker ran out of cash, suspended payment and went bankrupt.

The night of October 22, 1907, saw most of the bankers in New York—including Morgan—in conference. The United States Secretary of the Treasury, George Courtelyou, came to New York to help but the government had, in fact, little authority in this field. The next day another bank, the Trust Company of America, had depositors clamoring for their money—thirteen million dollars worth of it. But the Trust Company of America had help from other bankers, Morgan included, and it did not close. The Panic of 1907 continued—trading on the Pittsburgh Stock Exchange was suspended, prices of company shares tumbled as people hurried to get their hands on cash before

J. P. Morgan and other bankers came to each other's aid in 1907.

it was too late, there were more runs on different banks. But somehow the New York Stock Exchange remained open and disaster was avoided. Morgan and other bankers came to each other's aid. As one historian, Frederick Lewis Allen, puts it: "The lesson of the Panic of 1907 was clear. . . . The United States gravely needed a central banking system, which could build up reserves to be disposed of where they were most needed. The significance of Morgan's role during the panic was likewise clear. To the extent that a single man could exercise the functions of a central banking system, Morgan had done this. He had been, as it were, a one-man Federal Reserve Bank."

This big money panic set off government studies, including a congressional investigation carried out by the Pujo committee, named after Representative Arsene Pujo of Louisiana in 1913, and from these came the Federal Reserve Act of 1913. The Act set up the Federal Reserve system—a key factor in our monetary affairs and a very influential force in our general economy. It is not perfect or all-seeing or all-powerful. It did not, for instance, prevent the Great Depression of the 1930's. But it is a system that has developed through the years and has played an important part in the relatively stable and prosperous period following World War II.

The first thing to note about the Federal Reserve network is that it is peculiarly American in being part government and part private enterprise. The private enterprise part consists of the nation's most important commercial banks, some sixty-three hundred of them, which are members of the system, have capital stock in it, keep deposits at the Federal Reserve District Banks and have the right to borrow from them.

At the top of the Federal Reserve system is its Board of Governors—seven men appointed from the fields of banking, business, and agriculture by the President of the United States for fourteen-year terms. The appointments are staggered, normally a new one every two years. The chairman of the board is appointed, also by the President, from among the governors. He serves four-year renewable terms. William McChesney Martin, Jr., has had a long career in this office—he was first named chairman of the "Fed" in 1951. Martin's father helped draft the Federal Reserve Act back in 1913. And the son is a former "boy wonder," a tennis-playing Wall Street banker who was the first paid head of the New York Stock Exchange at the age of 31.

The board is a government agency, its members government employees, paid government salaries. But the long terms its members serve help give it independence and separate it from the mainstream of our political life. So does the fact that its operating funds do not come from money appropriated by Congress from the taxpayer's dollar. Its money comes from assessments on the twelve Federal Reserve banks. Each of these twelve has a fixed territory. There's one for New England, another for New York and New Jersey, and so forth. The largest is No. 12. It takes in some of the mountain states, all of the West Coast, and Alaska and Hawaii.

The twelve Federal Reserve banks are mixed institutions. They are owned by the member banks under strict conditions. They earn a profit but only a small portion of it may be paid to these owners. The rest is paid into the United States Treasury and thus the Federal Reserve system *saves* the taxpayer a few dollars, rather than the reverse.

The sixty-three hundred member banks throughout the country make up slightly less than one-half the existing commercial banks, but these Federal Reserve member banks include all national banks and they hold more than four-fifths of all commercial banking assets and deposits.

What does this rather complicated system do? The "Fed" says that its "chief responsibility is to regulate the flow of money and credit in order to promote economic stability and growth." Or, to put it another way, "Fed" officials speak of three objectives: "A high level of employment, stability in the over-all price level and an environment geared to a growing economy."

How does the "Fed" regulate the money supply? To find this out, we have to look first at some typical business transactions to get some idea of what happens to "bank-created money," or "checkbook money."

Consider what happens in our interlinked banking system when a businessman seeks a loan for, let us say, adding a new wing to his factory. If the banker approves the project as a sound one (sound and secured by collateral to the extent the banker feels assured he will get the bank's money back), the loan is granted. The businessman, for his part, rarely takes his borrowed money away as cash. Instead, he gets from the banker a bank account with the amount of the loan credited to it—and a checkbook with which to draw against this money. And the businessman uses his checks to pay the bills as they come in for the construction of the new factory space. When he pays his bills for real estate, for construction and the like, the chances are that his checks will be deposited either in the same bank or one linked to it.

The money in the bank continues to do a lot of work without ever leaving—or without leaving for very long. As the construction company working on the new factory pays *its* bills, it will also take care of most of them by check. A few decades ago, most of its wages to its employees would have been paid in cash; today the company may pay by check instead. In any case the workers will cash most of their checks. But the money won't stay out of the banks long. When the workers spend it in the supermarkets and stores, it will come back as deposits to the account of the companies and businessmen who operate these establishments. Ultimately, the new factory will be built and will be selling its products to these same supermarkets and stores. Then the businessman who originally borrowed to build the factory will be getting checks in payment—and depositing them to the account he originally opened with a loan from the bank. He in turn can pay off the loan with checks against this newly fortified account.

Now, consider how the Federal Reserve system *regulates* this process. The banks are not free to make as many loans as they like. They are required by law to protect the interests of their depositors. Therefore, the loans must be sound ones—almost certain to be repaid. But beyond that, the Federal Reserve lays down rules designed to regulate the flow of this checkbook money. One basic rule is that for every one hundred dollars it has deposited in its checking accounts, each member bank must deposit fifteen dollars—on the average—with its Federal Reserve district bank. And this has a fundamental effect on the nation's credit and money supply. Remember that few dollars leave the banking system for very long. Suppose, after receiving a $100 deposit a member bank deposits the required $15 with its district bank. It can then lend someone $85. If this is in the form of a new checking account—as most loans are—the $85 now counts as a deposit. The bank must now place another $12.75 (15 per cent of $85) with its reserves at the district bank. Now it can make a further loan of $72.25. And so forth. By this process each dollar of new deposits may become $6.66 in credit.

This ability to stretch a dollar in deposits to more than six in credit is part of the business of having an "elastic money supply"—a supply that fits the country's business needs and helps its economic growth.

The Federal Reserve has ways of controlling the elasticity—influencing just how much give and stretch there is. For one thing, it can change the legal reserve requirements. Instead of requiring that fifteen dollars of every one hundred on deposit be sent in to the reserve system, it can decree fourteen or sixteen.

This power is not used very often because there are two other important methods—rather technical and sophisticated, to be sure—for doing much the same thing.

One of these arises from the fact that the Federal Reserve buys and sells government bonds and other government securities. These "open market operations," as they are called, are tricky but interesting. Say the Federal Reserve *buys* a U.S. government bond worth one thousand dollars. The investor who previously owned the bond now has a thousand dollars. What does he do with it? He deposits it in a bank. And as we have just seen, this thousand dollars can build its way up to more than six thousand dollars worth of credit.

Conversely, when the Federal Reserve *sells* a bond it is pulling money out of circulation and restricting the money supply.

The Federal Reserve also lends money to its member banks, usually with the member banks pledging government securities as collateral. The interest rate that the Federal Reserve charges for these loans—known as the "discount rate"—is an influential factor in all other lending transactions in the economy. If the banks pay the Federal Reserve 4 per cent, they will charge their borrowers 4.5 per cent, or more. When the Federal Reserve lowers its interest rate, the commercial banks are able to lower their rates; when it raises the ante, so must the commercial banks. And the cost of borrowing a dollar, the price of using someone else's money, is important to the state of business at any given moment.

6 / INFLATION, DEFLATION, AND PROSPERITY

IN THE AUTUMN OF 1929 a good many American investors were wondering about the soundness of the prices of the stocks they held—whether, after the long, sometimes sudden rises of the previous years, they represented realistic values. Or whether they might begin to fall. And many of these investors owed money on their stock; they had bought their shares "on margin," that is, with funds borrowed from brokers, with the stock pledged against the debt. In those days it was possible to borrow as much as 90 per cent of the market value of the stock. After all, stocks were supposed to represent real wealth; brokers, banks, and other financial institutions regarded them as good collateral for such loans. And this meant that investors and speculators had a good thing going, that is, as long as the price of stocks kept going up as they had generally done throughout the 1920's.

Consider how it worked: you put up $100 of your own

money, borrowed $900, and bought 100 shares of High Flyer, Inc., at $10 a share for a total cost of $1,000. High Flyer, Inc., thereupon rose 25 cents a share one day, perhaps $1 a share another, to climb to $20 a share, whereupon you could sell out for $2,000. After paying off your loan of $900, you had a nice profit of $1,000 for an investment of $100. Now you had enough capital to borrow $9,000—all you needed was a tip on another stock that would climb upward as High Flyer had done.

In rational times stock prices rise because of improvements in the business prospects, competitive efficiency, and earning capacity of the companies they represent. Investors, buying shares on the stock market, bid up their price because they expect the firms to make more profits, enabling them to pay out bigger dividends—the rewards that the owners of the shares receive as a return for their investment. In rational times, company earnings and the price of their shares have a distinct relationship. But the 1920's were not rational in this regard. Prices spiraled upward in dizzying fashion simply because of the speculative fever and easy credit. A few successful ventures like the High Flyer episode and suddenly there were a host of people borrowing money, looking for favored stocks, bidding one against the other and raising the price of these stocks and hardly heeding the profit-and-loss accounts of the companies involved. Business would keep getting better and better, the assumption ran, and the earning capacity of the companies would catch up to the

VARIETY

PRICE 25¢

Published Weekly at 154 West 46th St., New York, N. Y., by Variety, Inc. Annual subscription, $10. Single copies, 25 cents.
Entered as second-class matter December 22, 1905, at the Post Office at New York, N. Y., under the act of March 3, 1879.

VOL. XCVII. No. 3   NEW YORK, WEDNESDAY, OCTOBER 30, 1929   88 PAGES

WALL ST. LAYS AN EGG

Going Dumb Is Deadly to Hostess In Her Serious Dance Hall Profesh

A hostess at Roseland has her problems. The paid steppers consider their work a definite profession calling for specialized technique and high-power salesmanship.

"You see, you gotta sell your personality," said one. "Each one of us girls has our own clientele to cater to. It's just like selling dresses in a store—you have to know what to sell each particular customer.

"Some want to dance, some want to kid, some want to get soupy, and others are just 'misunderstood husbands.'"

Girls applying for hostess jobs at Roseland must be 21 or older. They must work five nights a week. They are strictly on their own, no salary going with the job and the house collecting 10 cents on every $3 cent ticket. To keep her job, a girl must turn in at least 100 tickets a week during the cold season and $6 in the summer months. In a dull week girls buy their own tickets to keep up the record.

If a partner wishes to sit out a dance, he must pay for the privilege. "Sitting-out time" sells at eight tickets an hour, or $2.80. It's usually a poor sport who will come across with less than $3, many kicking in heavier for a little genial conversation.

The girl who knows her professional dancing trade will keep an alert eye open for potential "sitter-outers," ascertain their hobbies and talk herself into a whole string of tickets. In this way she not only earns money easily, but saves wear and tear on her evening dresses and slippers.

Big money rolls in if she has a good line. One of the most successful girls at Roseland takes this part of her work so seriously that she reads up on current events (sports and stock market included) and has a smattering of current literature and art.

"There are two types of hostesses at Roseland," she said, displaying high brow leanings. "They are the mental and the 'physical.' Surprisingly enough the physical ones are not those who make the most money. One customer will buy three tickets from me at the most. They rely on their sex appeal and go dumb between dances—and that's the surest way to lose a partner, going dumb.

Mental Girls

Hunk on Winchell

When the Walter Winchells moved into 204 West 55th street, late last week, June, that's Mrs. Winchell, selected a special room as Walter's exclusive sleep den for his late hour nights. She shushed the Winchell kiddies when her husband dove in at his usual eight o'clock the first morning.

At noon, Walter's midnight, his sound proof room was penetrated by so many high C's he awoke with but four hours of dreams and a grouch. Investigated at once, after having signed the lease of course.

Right next door, on the same floor, is the studio of the noted vocal instructor, Kinney. Among his pupils are Ona Munson, Irene Delroy and Marjorie Peterson. They love Winchell like you love carbolic acid.

And Miss Munson is reported to have requested that an amplifier be started hereafter when she runs up the scale.

Demand for Vaude

Springfield, Ill., Oct. 29.

Petitions requesting Publix theatres to resume vaudeville in Decatur, Ill. are in circulation in that city.

Petitions specify that vaudeville at one or more of the three larger Publix houses would furnish employment to a number of Decatur musicians and stage hands and provide larger variety of local entertainment.

Paul Witte, Publix manager in Decatur, states that he believes vaudeville will find a place in Decatur before the season is over.

Pickpocketing Dying Out

Chicago, Oct. 29.

Some 1,000-odd pickpockets who used to make Chicago what it was are no more. A confidential list in the hands of government revenue

DROP IN STOCKS ROPES SHOWMEN

Many Weep and Call Off Christmas Orders — Legit Shows Hit

MERGERS HALTED

The most dramatic event in the financial history of America is the collapse of the New York Stock Market. The stage was Wall Street, but the onlookers covered the country. Estimates are that 22,000,000 people were in the market at the time.

Tragedy, despair and ruination spell the story of countless thousands of marginal stock traders. Perhaps Manhattan was worst hit in the number of victims. Many may remain broke for the rest of their lives, because the money that disappeared via the ticker tape was the savings of years.

Many people of Broadway are known to have been wiped out. Reports of some in show business losing as much as $300,000 is not hearsay. One caustic comment to that was that the theatre is enough of a gamble without its people to venture into Wall street.

Prominent showmen, several identified with the picture industry
(Continued on page 84)

FILTHY SHOW OF SHUBERTS GOOD FOR SCREEN

Chicago, Oct. 29.

Shubert's latest musical of the "Night" series, now in Chicago, is so filthy that one of the cast admits embarrassment while in the performance.

The second act of this scramble called "Broadway Nights," is
(Continued on page 63)

Kidding Kissers in Talkers Burns Up Fans of Screen's Best Love

Talker Crashes Olympus

Paris, Oct. 29.

Fox "Follies" and the Fox Movietone newsreel are running this week in Athens, Greece, the first sound pictures heard in the birthplace of world culture, and in all Greece, for that matter.

Several weeks ago, Variety's Cairo correspondent cabled that a cinema had been wired in Alexandria, Cleopatra's home town.

Only Sodom and Gomorrah remain to be heard from.

HOMELY WOMEN SCARCE: CAN'T EARN OVER $25

No homely ones on Broadway!

And now it looks as if Crosby Gaige may have to postpone production of "One Beautiful Evening" because the Main Stem is devoid of the non-beauties necessary for the casting of the show.

Arthur Lubin, caster for the producer, for several weeks has been trying to land the right type of women. A most unusual piece, the drama has an all-women lineup, and, although as many as 25 are needed, all must be homely—and middle age or over, except for two who can be young.

Vera Caspary wrote the play and it centers about conditions at a club for girls where requirements of residence demand that the girls must not earn over $15 per week in order to live under its roof. That's why they must be homely.

Ads for Execs

Chicago, Oct. 29.

Newspaper ad calling for potential executives for the Publix-B. & K. organisation here, drew heavy response, with over 100 applicants.

Boys who used to whistle at girls who used to giggle when scenes were flashed on the screen are in action again. A couple years ago they began to talk love stuff seriously and don't but the talkers are reviving ha ha for film ossulators.

Heavy loving lovers of picture days accustomed to closing audiences into spasms of ecstasy when kissing the big lady are getting the bird in a commotion during a clinch.

Such a picture romancer as Gilbert is getting laughs in the sight of other days, as the flaps who still think he's great are getting sore. One little flap to be quieted by an onlooker during a commotion during a clinch at the Capitol, New York. The person sitting next to her many others in the house, Gilbert's passion lightly. They jumped to his defense and started to bawl out the Gilbert detractor.

Not only has Gilbert received bird lately, but all of the other screen players who specialize in romance. Charley Farrell in "Sunny Side Up" draws many a razz from his most rabid fans.

In the silents when a star would whisper like a ventriloquist his lips apart and unmoved, as his eyes passionately probed to the clinch and then kissed pretty natural and unbreakable. The build-up to the kissing now makes a gag of the kiss.

When the kiss is with intent, the laughs are out of it. It's burning the Impassioned fans to see their favorite riddled when kissing.

In Reverse

Seems the only type of love received as intended since of the talkers in the comedy scene. The screen comics coming the heavy lovers of heavy lovers comedians.

The normal kiss, delivered the usual smack, sounds like plosion. For that reason scenes in the early talkers draw rolling in the aisles.

Tuning down their kissing make it senseless has continued the noyer's best kissers of the screen's best, but, audible or silent, they are getting laughs that belong long.

Variety announces the crash to its readers. A few weeks later, thirty billion dollars' worth of paper values had disappeared.

high "paper values"—based on the projections of future operations—at which stock market transactions were taking place.

But there were grim dangers involved in all the stock owned "on margin"—on credit—in 1929. While brokers and other lenders put up their funds for 90 per cent of the value of stock held in an individual's account, they had to act if the market value of the stock fell below that point. Then the borrower was called on to put up more cash to cover his margin. And if he didn't put up this cash, the broker could—and did—sell the pledged stock to recover as much as the debt owed him as possible. In the fall of 1929 prudent investors, reviewing business prospects, the precarious nature of prices being paid for stock and the amount of debt outstanding, began to sell stock. Prices, naturally, dropped a little. Then uneasiness grew, so that even the less prudent took alarm and did the same. As more people sold their shares, it became increasingly difficult to find buyers unless bargain prices were offered. As prices slid lower, pessimism grew and the urge to sell grew stronger. On the morning of October 24, 1929, it seemed that everyone wanted to sell, no one wanted to buy, and the sharpest drop—"the crash"—began. The brokers, watching the diminishing market value of the stocks on which they had lent money, called upon their customers to put up more money. These "margin calls," in many cases, could not be met—and the brokers dumped the pledged shares on the market, too, to salvage their claims, adding more rolling stones to the landslide. Unhappy, often desperate speculators who had counted themselves rich watched their fortunes disappear. A few committed suicide, creating a not very accurate legend of broken financiers diving from the windows of their Wall Street skyscrapers to end it all.

In a few weeks thirty billion dollars of paper values disappeared—a colossal amount in relation to the size of the economy of the time. The crash was followed by the Great Depression, an era that proved several things rather conclusively. One was that the world economy was in fact an entity—that it was most difficult to separate one country's depression from another. And the second was the destructive effects of falling prices, or deflation, on a nation's economic health and growth.

Today, when war and international conflict have had an almost continuous effect on the United States economy for more than twenty-five years, we have come to think almost exclusively in terms of inflation—rising prices—and what must be done to keep inflation from having adverse effects. And we sometimes forget just why we have built a number of bulwarks and protective devices to prevent abruptly declining prices. But in the 1930's the destructive effects of falling prices could be seen everywhere. What had happened in the stock market was a very, very sharp change in the way many Americans assessed the value of their factories and business organizations. Take the case of one of the nation's biggest companies, United States Steel. One day in September 1929 investors, through their bidding and buying and selling

of shares, valued the assets of this company—its ore deposits, blast furnaces, steel mills and all the elements of its
productive capacity—so that its stock sold at $262 a share.
A thousand shares were worth $262,000. But just a little
more than two months later—after the October crash—
the shares had slid to a low of $167 a share, and any one
holding a thousand shares had lost almost $100,000. The
investing public, in its buying and selling at the trading
posts of the New York Stock Exchange, valued the same
amount of physical assets, the business ability of the company's managers and the firm's prospects by that much
less. But 1929 was not the worst of the story, by any
means. The descent continued downward and less than
three years later a share of the U.S. Steel could be bought
for $22; those assets that had once been valued at more
than a quarter of a million dollars could be had for $22,-
000. And the same thing had happened to real estate,
houses, and farms—in some cases to an even greater extent.

Consider what this meant. The company directors of
the XYZ Corporation, let us say, were in the midst of
building a widget factory. All their calculations were
based on the idea that they could manufacture widgets
at less than one dollar each and then sell them profitably
at $1—the going rate for widgets at the time. These calcu-
lations included the value of the land the company directors had bought to build their factory on, the cost of
construction, the wages they expected to pay skilled
widget-makers, the commissions they would pay their

salesmen and a host of other factors. Like most businesses of that day and this, they had borrowed money to buy the land and build the factory, and so their calculations included provisions for paying interest on the borrowed funds and for repaying the debt itself. Now, suddenly, all their calculations were wrong, and they knew it and their creditors knew it. The land they had paid $20,000 for was now worth perhaps $5,000. The factory they had already spent $75,000 to build could not be sold for half that amount. They owed $60,000 for assets that now could be bought for less than $20,000. And even if they went ahead with the plans for widget-making—saving perhaps on lower wages for their workers and lower costs for raw materials—they were faced with the fact that widgets were now selling for 60 cents, and might easily sink to 50 cents or 40 cents as established widget-makers intensified their competition in a dwindling market.

Better go slow, said the president of the XYZ Corporation, better see what the market for widgets is going to be. As a consequence of this decision to go slow, the widget factory never opened, the jobs that would have been created by the new factory just didn't materialize, and wage-earners who might have been out buying widgets and other consumer goods were not buying much of anything but the bare necessities of life.

Because of the universality of this business pessimism, there was sudden talk of overproduction—that is, overproduction in terms of consumers with money available to buy. Too many goods were chasing too little money in

the economic merry-go-round. Prices of goods were falling; it was better to hold on to cash, because it was certain that a dollar would buy more tomorrow than it did
today. Money was precious, dear; goods, labor, and property were suddenly cheap.

In the 1930's, falling prices were a curse that not only
kept factories from opening, but also reduced farmers
to despair as they tried to market their crops on a market
that kept offering them less and less for their work. Deflation was an especially paralyzing blow to the construction industry. In Miami, Florida, where the bubble of
inflated values had been greatest, big office buildings were
abandoned half-finished, their steel skeletons standing un-
touched because no one could realistically foresee a demand for them. What accentuated the calamity all the
more was the nation's collective debt—mortgages on
houses, bank loans to businesses, credit to farmers. The
positions of debtors and creditors in the wake of dras-

In Miami buildings were abandoned half finished.

tically revised public assessment of property values were almost equally hopeless. Men whose businesses had failed, jobless workers, poorer farmers just couldn't make payment on their mortgages on house, farm, or business premise. And what is more, there wasn't much point in trying to pay off a $10,000 mortgage on a house which, it was becoming apparent, was worth a good deal less. It seemed better to let the bank foreclose, many people decided. And that was how bankers found themselves in the real estate business, with many properties unmarketable for years to come.

But the most drastic, destructive, and self-perpetuating feature of the economic contraction that went on in the United States and many other parts of the world in the 1930's was unemployment. When businesses faced nothing but losses, when farmers were going broke by the hundreds, they just didn't hire people. New factories didn't open, old ones closed, building came to a halt, and more and more people lost their jobs.

No one knows for sure how many unemployed Americans there were at that time but government estimates now put the total at thirteen million at the peak, at a time when there were about fifty-two million people in the labor force. In the bleak year of 1933 one out of every four workers was unemployed. A nation capable of creating so much was having trouble making ends meet, was confused, muddled, in the midst of one of the most puzzling man-made periods of stagnation ever known.

This was the reverse of Germany's runaway inflation

after World War I, but it was no less mad and destructive. Naturally all kinds of remedies were tried in an attempt to find a cure for this rash of falling prices. They included devaluing our currency, public works projects, price supports for agricultural products, the National Industrial Recovery Act (which was something of a price-fixing attempt), minimum wage laws, and the like. Not all of them worked; others have become a permanent part of our present economic life.

During the 1930's people began to talk about the ideas of an Englishman, John Maynard Keynes. Keynes was a Cambridge professor, ballet lover, sometime speculator in foreign currencies, director of an insurance company and very articulate critic of such public figures as Woodrow Wilson and Winston Churchill. Before Keynes, many economists focused attention on the automatic operation of supply and demand. If there was unemployment, they said, wages would fall until it became profitable for a businessman to hire more people and put them to work making useful goods. Savings, investments, interest rates—all part of the pattern of employment and production—would also move automatically. The government, these economists said, should not intervene; it should set a good example by balancing its own expenditures against its income from taxation.

The trouble was that in the 1930's this didn't work. And Keynes said as much in a famous open letter to President Franklin D. Roosevelt published in *The New York Times* on December 31, 1933. He spoke about the role of purchasing power—who could buy what—in the economy. And he stressed the government's ability to hire and to buy, even if it had to borrow heavily to do so.

"As a prime mover in the first stage of the technique of recovery," he wrote, "I lay overwhelming emphasis on the increase of national purchasing power resulting from governmental expenditure which is financed by loans and is not merely a transfer through taxation from existing income. Nothing else counts in comparison with this." The government, he argued, could balance its budget in the good years, when employment was high, and could then swing back the other way when employment declined. This, he said, was the road to stability.

His ideas were heatedly debated at the time—and for many years afterward. His critics spoke about "deficit financing" and predicted national bankruptcy. But some people think Keynes was the most influential economist of this century, that he offered the most effective answer to an influential economist of a century earlier, Karl Marx. In essence, Keynes was saying that major economic swings—the cycle of prosperity and depression—in free economies could be counterbalanced and controlled. His theories did not by any means end the Great Depression in the United States or elsewhere. But the circumstances that did bring an end to the depression—the coming of World War II—demonstrated a number of things about his theories.

For it was government enterprise of the biggest kind —the national effort needed to fight and win the war—

As more and more people lost their jobs, some turned to selling apples in large cities.

that set America working at full capacity. Before the war
ended, the nation had had the experience of full employment, even of housewives working as riveters in aircraft
plants, of regular weekly paychecks, of what came to be
called a miracle of production. This side of the picture,
everyone agreed, was desirable. But there was another
side that was worrisome. Taxes were higher and more
people had to pay them. Even so, the national debt
soared. In 1929 it was some sixteen billion dollars; by
1940 it was fifty billion dollars—a sizeable increase. But
by 1945 it was almost $280 billion, a truly staggering sum
far beyond anything Keynes had in mind when he was
urging government borrowing during the first stage of
recovery.

What was the real significance of such a large debt?
Some people regarded it as a frightening, almost intoler-
able burden. They pointed out that, at that time, it was
greatly in excess of the value of the total yearly output
of all the mines and factories and business establishments
in the country—which is referred to by economists as the
gross national product. That meant it was debt that
couldn't be paid off even if everyone worked for nothing
for a year. And, because people have to eat and consume
some of the products of their labor in order to live, that
meant it would be generations before such a debt could
be repaid.

Nonetheless, it could not be said that the nation was
actually bankrupt. It was even possible to show that
America was more wealthy than before the war. It had,

for instance, a good many new factories built with borrowed funds. As the war ended and the economy switched over to civilian production, it also began to have other items that unmistakably represented real wealth—houses, office buildings, new automobiles, refrigerators, television sets, schools, hospitals, and other durable, useful things that could be expected to fulfill their function for years to come.

In any case, despite the national debt, the country was in a mood to continue working at full capacity—at a high rate of employment. And Congress, taking a fresh look at the economy and the government's role in it, passed a law known as the Employment Act of 1946. This called for the development of "economic policies to foster and promote free competitive enterprise, to avoid economic fluctuations or to diminish the effects thereof." It also set forth as a government aim the promotion of "maximum employment, production and purchasing power." It established a Council of Economic Advisers to report to and assist the President in achieving these aims. And it established a Joint Senate-House of Representatives Committee to consider and review what the Executive Branch does in this field.

Thereafter, each year the President has submitted an annual economic report, supplemented by a report by the Council of Economic Advisers, and each year the Joint Economic Committee has studied these documents and reported on this and its own reading of the American economic situation.

This yearly procedure by itself does not ensure either sound money, full employment, or increased production. But what it does do is to bring together, for annual review by a number of experts, all the considerable economic powers that the federal government now has. This includes what the Treasury is doing about paying interest, retiring old bonds and selling new ones. It includes what the Federal Reserve Board is doing about the influential factors of credit and the money supply. And, in recent years, there have been increasing efforts to establish a sound balance between what the government takes in in revenue and what it pays out in expenditure—the Keynesian formula of control.

There is more agreement among economists now that the right balance depends on the state of the economy in any given year. Postwar experience has shown some interesting things about government actions. For instance, a sizeable income tax cut under President Eisenhower in 1954 did not bring about as big a reduction in federal revenue as might have been expected. In fact, within two years, the new tax at the lower rate was bringing in more revenue than the old, higher rate had done. The reason: the economy itself had grown in the meanwhile; more people were making more money and the government's share amounted to a bigger total.

An important part of the story was that the tax cut itself had helped stimulate the growth. When tax-payers found themselves with more take-home pay, they did a very natural thing—they spent more. And their added spending was reflected in the income of auto-makers, restaurant owners, department store operators who, in turn, spent more to hire additional workers, and so forth. This chain reaction, according to the economists, is a "multiplier effect"—ten dollars worth of tax cut can amount to forty dollars worth of increase in the country's total expenditure.

Obviously, such a process is a valuable tool for spurring along a lagging economy. Within limits, it is a way of having one's cake and eating it too; that is, it may be possible to cut taxes without lowering government income or incurring a federal budget deficit.

The possibilities intrigued President Kennedy. At the beginning of his administration, he wanted Congress to give the President the power to reduce income tax rates, within fixed limits, at times of economic need and subject to a congressional veto. Congress, however, guards its power to set tax rates, and Mr. Kennedy later turned his suggestion into a request for a straight tax cut as a method of bringing the rate of unemployment—almost 7 per cent in 1961—down to 4 per cent. After the Kennedy assassination, President Johnson argued vigorously for the tax cut and got it. The results were evident in 1964. The cut, the biggest ever, pumped some twelve billion dollars worth of spending power into the economy; total output rose by about $40 billion as the multiplier effect did its work. One and one-half million new jobs were created. And government revenue, instead of falling, rose.

Many of the experts regard this experience as proof that

a "Keynesian Revolution" has shown ways of regulating the economy so that it performs smoothly and prosperously. In fact, a number of economists and businessmen sharply criticized President Johnson in 1966 because he did not seek a tax increase for the purpose of "dampening" the economy, keeping it from "overheating"—that is, suppressing its inflationary tendencies. Not every one, of course, subscribes to the Keynesian theory. They tend to reject its emphasis on government intervention. Prosperity, they say, depends on private enterprise, its freedom of operation, business confidence, monetary stability, and the rise and fall of prices.

In their efforts to establish more jobs and ensure healthy industrial growth, most of America's modern economic managers keep a close eye on prices—on the various ways of measuring how much or how little our money will buy. History has taught the dangers of large and sudden deflation and inflation alike. Persistent, gradual small-scale inflation—gentle year-by-year price rises—does not seem to endanger the economy, but it too has its disadvantages. It penalizes bondholders and other lenders—the fixed amount of dollars they lend are worth more in terms of goods at the time of lending than at the time of repayment. Pensioners and people who save for retirement are affected the same way; the money put away during their years of work may have less purchasing power in later years when they have stopped working.

In any case, there is a staggering array of statistics by

which to gauge the purchasing power of the dollar from one era to another.

The Bureau of Labor Statistics issues the *Consumer Price Index* and the *Wholesale Price Index*. Statisticians prepare an index of this kind by figuring out the average prices of a set of goods year by year. Then they select a base period—an average, say, for the three years 1963, 1964 and 1965—and specify that prices in that period represent 100. Then if prices go up 10 per cent the next year, the index for that year stands at 110. If they drop 10 per cent, the index will fall to 90.

The best known of these indexes is the *Consumer Price Index*, sometimes called the "cost of living index," although this is not quite accurate. This tells us something about the changes in the prices paid by the families of wage-earners and clerical workers in cities across the nation. Statisticians have actually drawn up a shopping list of the breakfast cereals, butter, eggs and meat, the shirts and ties and dresses that these families buy. And month by month they check the actual prices of some three hundred representative items, carefully ascertaining that the quality of the goods stays pretty much the same. They also check on rents and the cost of housing to home-owners, on electric bills, bus fares, and the expenses of owning a car, on doctor's bills, the price of dry cleaning, and even the cost of beauty parlor treatment. The index goes back to 1913 but there have been many refinements since it was started. For instance, the list of items it represents has been changed from time to time as America's living habits have changed. The price of new and used cars didn't mean too much to the city dweller of the 1920's, nor did the cost of a television set. But they play a big part in today's index. Even so, the *Consumer Price Index* doesn't measure the true cost of living for everyone. It doesn't take account of the price of diamonds or champagne, of jet flights to Paris and other of the items that might go into a millionaire's budget. It may not be representative for the extremely frugal person who avoids onetime luxuries that some of us now accept as routine— things we can't possibly do without—frozen foods, for instance.

The *Consumer Price Index* doesn't deal with the prices paid by farmers for things they need, for equipment, livestock, or feed grain, for instance. There is a Department of Agriculture index for that. The *Consumer Price Index* is frankly a city dweller's index, but even here only for those city dwellers who work in factories and shops for wages or earn salaries at clerical jobs. The experts say it gives a good picture of the ebb and flow of spending power for about 64 per cent of the nation's urban population—or for about 40 per cent of the total population.

Still, it is a good measure of the prices that we must pay for many of the things we need, or think we need. And as such, it is a way of measuring the changing value of our money. For when the cost of living goes up, the value—the usefulness—of each dollar of our money goes down. And when the cost of living goes down, each dollar buys more bread and butter, shoe leather, kilowatts of electricity, or jelly beans.

When the cost of living rises from 100 to 110, it means that the purchasing power of the dollar has shrunk 10 per cent. When it goes from 100 down to 90, it means that the dollar will buy 10 per cent more. Sometimes, when prices rise people talk about a 90-cent dollar or a 60-cent dollar because the dollar at the new price level will buy only what the lesser sum used to buy. The figures may seem confusing, but the idea is simple enough: the purchasing power of money changes from time to time.

For many years now, the *Consumer Price Index* has been moving in one direction—up. But looking back to the time of the Wall Street crash and the Great Depression the downward movement during that period is very clear. Using 1947–49 as the base period when the index equaled 100, prices in 1929 stood at 73. By 1933 the index slumped to 55—a decrease of almost 25 per cent. It was not until the wartime year of 1943 that the index climbed back to the 1929 level. World War II, of course, set in motion classic inflationary forces—heavy government spending on arms, high wages in defense industries, and full employment. At the same time there were not enough consumer goods in the shops. Inevitably, there was too much money chasing too few goods—the economist's favorite explanation of inflation. During the war the effects were suppressed by such special devices as price controls and rationing accompanied by the patriotic fervor that made people want to observe them. But after the war when controls were quickly discarded the price index jumped twenty points in the years 1946 and 1947. And the next big jump—nine points—came between 1950 and 1951 with the beginning of the Korean War. Aside from these abrupt changes, the United States record for rising prices in the postwar era has not been particularly alarming, at least not when judged by the records of other nations. Inflation has occurred in steps of one, two, three, or four points a year, sometimes less. Once it was only one-half a percentage point; another time, between 1954 and 1955, it retreated three-tenths of a point.

President Johnson, addressing himself to this question in a 1966 news conference, noted that the average increase in the *Consumer Price Index* since World War II was 2.6 per cent. He pointed out that, starting with 1960 as 100, the index for 1966 was 108, an 8 per cent increase. And then he compared this with other large, relatively stable industrial countries. For Federal Germany a similar index stood at 117, for Great Britain, it was 121, for France 122, for Italy 129, and for Japan 139.

Even beyond this, there are comparisons that would be difficult to calculate statistically—those that would show the drastic declines in the purchasing power of such unstable currencies as the Brazilian cruzeiro and the Indonesian rupiah. In contrast with these, the *Consumer Price Index* makes the American dollar look like a rock of Gibraltar in international monetary affairs.

7 / MANAGING MONEY

WHEN PRICES GO UP and down, when there is chaotic buying and selling on the stock market, when the experts are arguing about the possibilities of a recession and the dangers of inflation, it is hard for the average citizen to tell what action he, as an individual, should take. Yet all of us are affected by the crosscurrents and prevailing winds of our economic climate. We can sell a car, buy a house, or even choose a trade or profession at "the right time" or "the wrong time." We recognize that property values in residential areas may go down when a big, unsightly factory is built nearby. It is not wise to expect many job opportunities in declining or static industries—such as railroading, coal mining, textiles, or farming. There is even a "wrong time" to save money. During periods of inflation, its buying power grows smaller and smaller, and it will therefore buy less when it is withdrawn from the bank than when it was deposited. A man with keen economic foresight, sensing inflation ahead, buys real estate in what he hopes will become the most desirable neighborhood in town. Or he turns his money into something likely to be of lasting value—diamonds, for instance—anticipating the likelihood that they will be worth more later, in terms of deteriorating money, than when they were bought. A man, sensing deflation, on the other hand, will do exactly the opposite. He will sell his real estate and jewels and keep money, that is, cash or forms of money similar to cash, such as bank deposits and savings bonds.

Of course, the man with *perfect* economic foresight does not exist; in real situations it is extremely difficult to forecast that property values will actually go down when a factory is built; declining industries sometimes make a comeback; and inflation can turn, rather suddenly, into deflation, or vice versa. Moreover, even when trends persist, individuals—hardy, determined, and enduring, or sometimes just plain lucky—can buck the trend and make a success of the most unlikely looking projects.

Obviously, then, there is no magic formula for accumulating wealth, no sure way to manage money so that it is always growing. But there are ways to minimize risks, to balance one kind of an investment with another so that there is diversification, so that neither inflation nor deflation will bring disaster. All of us manage our money, whether it is a little or a lot, whether we do it badly or well. We can pinpoint one chronic money problem in a few words—not enough of it.

Mr. Micawber tells David Copperfield: "Annual income, twenty pounds, annual expenditure nineteen nineteen six, result happiness. Annual income twenty pounds, annual expenditure twenty ought six, result misery.

And in fact, one of the most common questions put to financial counselors is: How do I get started, where do I get my first nest egg? The most obvious answer is an old-fashioned one: thrift. Playwright George Bernard Shaw once noted that capital is spare cash, a truism so simple it is worth jotting down. The way to get spare cash is to spend a little less than you take in. Novelist Charles Dickens summed it up when he had Mr. Micawber give David Copperfield this advice: "Annual income twenty pounds, annual expenditure nineteen nineteen six, result happiness. Annual income twenty pounds, annual expenditure twenty ought six, result misery." Happiness,

according to Dickens, was living on a rather meager
Victorian income and saving sixpence a year. It is notable
that he did nothing of the kind himself. He was a
spender. But as literary success came along, Dickens
solved the chronic money problem the way most of us
would like to—he simply made more money, increasing
his income rather than curtailing his outgo.

There are many ways of increasing one's income. You
can write a best-seller, strike oil or gold in your back-
yard, invent a better mousetrap, or inherit a fortune from
a rich uncle. Most of us strive to do it in relatively pedes-
trian ways. We learn a trade, or go to a university to im-
prove our chances of getting a good job. We may
continue our education after we have started working;
we seek promotions or look around for a new job for the
same reason.

But even when we do this, we have to manage at the
same time with the money we have. Here the advice of
a Greek poet, Hesiod, adds to that offered David Copperfield. "If thou shouldst lay up even a little upon a little,
and shouldst do this often," Hesiod wrote, "soon would
even this become great."

Sixpence a year for Hesiod was not enough; it had to be
a little saved often enough. And here banks and bonds
and monthly savings plans take their cue.

One way of saving little by little, which we have al-
ready discovered in Chapter 4, is to accumulate U.S.
Savings Bonds, just about the safest way to earn interest.
The smallest units cost $18.75 each and are worth $25 at

maturity. These are one of the most versatile means of saving and investing. They can be made out to two persons, man and wife or parent and child, and cashed by either one. They can be held beyond the date of maturity, and the government will continue to pay interest on them. They are well worth having.

Savings accounts in regular banks and in savings and loan associations offer another opportunity for the thrifty. Look at the interest rate offered. For safety, look also for a statement that deposits are insured by an agency of the U.S. government. The Federal Deposit Insurance Corporation does this for regular banks and the Federal Savings and Loan Insurance Corporation does it for savings and loan associations. Not all savings institutions come under such a system, but the person who ignores this safety feature is usually taking a needless risk. The insurance covers accounts up to value of $15,000 each against the possibility of bank failure. Such insurance is another innovation added to our financial arrangements after the many bank failures during the Great Depression of the 1930's.

Many modern David Copperfields will want to learn something about life insurance. They will find that the earlier it is bought, the cheaper it is, and the easier it is for some one, as he grows older, to add new policies. Insurance salesmen will tell you that buying life insurance is a great way to save money. There is some truth in this, but the real value of insurance comes from its primary insurance function. It is protection against loss; it guarantees a certain sum of money to the dependents—wives and children—of a family wage-earner if he should die. Insurance companies charge for this protection and so the cash value of a policy is worth less than all the premiums that are paid in—whereas with a bank account interest adds to the total. Most breadwinners live long enough to see the children grow up, become educated, and go out and earn their own living. After this stage, there is less need for insurance, and a man who has reached retirement age may find he wants to take the cash value of some of his insurance policies. How much life insurance a person ought to have is impossible to judge without knowing his circumstances. If you are rich enough —in the millionaire class—life insurance may be of little real value. The inheritance a very wealthy man leaves behind makes insurance superfluous even after taxes. And during his lifetime, he usually takes care of his dependents with gifts, trust funds, and the like.

After putting by a little in the way of savings and *after* buying some life insurance, the modern young man in search of a fortune can think about common stock. This, of course, means putting money into a business venture— buying a share of it. There is a risk involved here—let there be no mistake about it. The risks are less than they were in the unregulated speculative days of the 1920's. There are laws restricting margin and other forms of credit. But even with such protection, the risks are there. The price of a share of stock, even of a well-known, large industrial firm, can drop substantially in a bewildering short span of days when the company's earnings fall off or when various kinds of adverse news affect the company's fortunes. On the other hand, such prices can also double, although the upswings usually take longer than the downswings. What makes common stocks desirable is their long-run trend upward in prosperous times. There is plenty of evidence that a sound investment in good stocks can literally make a man's fortune. There have been schoolteachers, restaurant workers, and other people of modest income who have managed, by buying a few shares here and a few shares there in a systematic savings and investing program, to build up estates of $100,000 or more. They have participated in the growth of enterprises like International Business Machines, Sears Roebuck, Eastman Kodak, American Telephone and Telegraph, and General Motors.

But it is the wise young man who starts slowly, and learns as he goes. One way to begin is with a mutual fund. This means buying shares in an investment company— a company which has no business of its own except for buying and selling shares in other firms. Such mutual funds are professionally managed by men who spend a great deal of time analyzing market trends and the records of individual companies. They usually buy shares in a fairly wide assortment of industries and individual firms, thus building up what is called a "diversified portfolio." The mutual fund collects the dividends on its investments and pays them to its owners. It also may distribute to these owners capital gains—that is, the profits that come

Trading on the New York Stock Exchange.

from buying a stock low and selling it high. It may have capital losses, but these will be reflected in a fall in the selling price of the mutual fund's own shares. The worth of its shares are calculated by figuring the worth of the stock it owns and dividing it by the number of shares it has outstanding in the hands of its owners. There are, of course, fees and salaries to be paid for the services of the mutual fund's professional managers, and these are taken out in various ways before the mutual fund owner reaps his full return.

Another important consideration is that most mutual funds are sold by salesmen, and their initial commission is a substantial charge on any short-lived account. A customer agrees to invest $100 a month in a mutual fund; the fund's affairs prosper, the stocks it holds increase in value; but when the customer wants to sell his fund shares a year later, he may find he has less than the amount he put in. The reason: the salesman's commission and other charges took all the gains. Obviously it is not a good idea to go into such an investment on a short-term basis. There are some mutual funds that do not have salesmen and therefore do not charge commissions; they are called "no-load" funds. They advertise and let the customers come to them. But, naturally enough, they are less well known and less patronized.

Mutual funds, for the most part, have been good investments over the past fifteen years. But that is because the stock market trend has been upward—the price of shares in many of the best companies has increased substantially. Investors who have bought such stocks directly, without the intermediary of a mutual fund, have done well too. The investor must ask himself whether he wants to have someone else do his selecting of stocks and charge a fee for it, or whether he wants to do it himself. In making such decisions, the modern David Copperfield will find plenty of people to advise him—brokers, mutual funds salesmen, and so forth. The one thing he should remember is that it is his money at stake; he alone will reap the gain or suffer the loss.

Managing one's money in today's world calls for some knowledge of how and when to borrow money. Shakespeare's advice—neither a borrower nor a lender be—may have its merits in personal relationships, but it does not apply elsewhere very widely in our affluent society. It is possible to be *both* a borrower and a lender without getting into undue difficulties. Well over half of all American families own their own homes, and nearly all of these homeowners have, or have had, mortgages to help them make the purchase. A great many Americans buy their automobiles on the installment plan; many buy furniture, refrigerators, washing machines, and a number of other things the same way. In all such cases, they have simply borrowed money to make the purchase, agreeing to pay it back so much per month. In all cases they are paying interest, often a great deal more interest than they realize.

Is this good or bad? It depends. It makes sense for most families to borrow money to buy a house because a house is a long-term investment. Most houses are built to last forty or fifty years; they can be renovated to last much longer. Paying interest, at 5.5 to 6.5 per cent, even though it represents a sizeable sum each year, may be a

worthwhile way of acquiring ownership of a valuable asset. Meanwhile, the family has the use of the house. If
the family did not live in its own house and pay interest
on its mortgage, it would have to live somewhere else
and pay rent. Such rent would represent most of the same
charges, including interest on money borrowed to build
the apartment house or the individual dwelling being
rented.

A house is an investment. Many of the other things
bought on borrowed money these days are used up fairly
quickly—they represent consumption. One of the fastest
types of consumption is that offered by the airlines: fly
now, pay later. There may be very good reasons for ac-
cepting this tempting offer on occasions, but the person
who does so should never fool himself into thinking he
is being frugal. Nor is the rate of interest he will pay
likely to be as reasonable as that for some other kinds of
borrowing. Banks and finance companies seek more security and charge higher rates when extending credit for
something that is to be used up before the money is paid
back.

For instance, take the person who goes to a bank or a
finance company and gets what looks like a 6 per cent
loan for $1,000 to buy a second-hand car. Let's say he is
willing to pay back the loan in a year. He has $1,060 to
pay back—the original $1,000 plus $60 in interest. Under
most installment contracts, he then makes his payments
in equal monthly installments. Isn't this 6 per cent in-

terest? Certainly not. Since he is paying his debt back from month to month, he doesn't have the use of the full $1,000 for the whole year. Rather, he has the use of an average of $500. And his true rate of interest, the mathematicians tell us, is 11 per cent, nearly double the 6 per cent that may have appeared on the advertisement.

Then there's the question of small interest rates for short periods of time—and how different they look when calculated on a yearly basis. Many department stores, for example, charge 1 per cent per month, or 1.5 per cent or 2 per cent per month, on the unpaid balance that a credit customer owes. Well, 1 per cent a month is 12 per cent a year; 1.5 per cent a month is 18 per cent a year; and 2 per cent a month is 24 per cent.

These days nearly everyone uses credit—for convenience and even safety, since a credit card can mean less cash to carry around. The plastic credit card, with its raised name and numbers, is, of course, a modern, almost revolutionary, form of money. Put the credit card—for spending—together with the checkbook—for paying— and an adventuresome person can travel around the world satisfying scores of consumer wants without ever touching a coin or a bill. One of the most prevalent kinds of credit cards are those issued by the oil companies. And the companies do not charge interest or fees for billing you once at the end of the month for what you buy. They know that once you have their credit card, you will be less likely to buy another brand of gasoline.

Many department stores use the credit card as a sales tool in the same fashion, charging no interest or fees on their short-term accounts. The more general credit cards issued by restaurant associations, hotel chains, or travel agencies involve a relatively small yearly fee. They also limit the buyer to the select group of sellers who honor each kind of card—and the customer may be paying higher prices by doing most of his buying within this group.

In any case, the credit card is definitely here to stay. Under the circumstances it is the wise modern David Copperfield who finds out how much and in what ways, direct or indirect, he is paying for his credit—so that he can do it with his eyes open and judge for himself whether he is getting his money's worth.

8 / TOWARD A WORLD MONEY

MANY AN INTERNATIONAL TRAVELER, in the confusion of exchanging currencies, has thought how convenient it would be to have a single world currency. Why do we have to bother with all the different kinds of money—British pounds, Italian lire, Burmese kyats, Spanish pesetas, Yugoslav dinars? Wouldn't it be much much simpler to have a United Nations *uno*?

The answer is: the world isn't ready for it. There seems no possibility at this time of a single world currency for the *entire* world—the Soviet Union, Communist China, the eastern European countries included. But if we consider the rest of the world—particularly the economically sound countries of America, Western Europe, and parts of Asia—then perhaps one can foresee an international currency. But even here the difficulties are formidable.

A single monetary unit would, of course, make it much more simple to buy and sell things; it would greatly increase world trade, help people to travel for business and pleasure, help them send funds to their relatives across international frontiers, help them to change jobs, and move from country to country to live.

The trouble is that not every one wants these things or wants to pay the price to achieve them. As we have seen, the value of our dollar depends on many factors, including its gold backing, the stability of our government, the government's skill at keeping prices stable and the economy strong, and the credit rating it has built up at home and abroad through the years.

At present there is no comparable organization to stand behind a world currency—no world government with a credit rating either good or bad. Nor is one in sight, for the United Nations, at the moment at least, does not have the necessary financial powers.

There are signs that most countries prefer this situation. They are accustomed to think in national terms, about national economies. They would object vigorously to an outsider controlling their money and all the vital things connected with it—taxes, jobs, trade, prices, and the like. As a result, today's international monetary arrangements are based on agreements among individual nations without one single authority to back them up. And there is always Gresham's law lurking in the background: bad money drives out good. This is an important consideration when pooling U.S. money with other currencies—there is always the danger that the dollar will lose value because of the association.

Still, the need for a world currency is real, and proposals

and debate about all kinds of new schemes are likely to go on for decades. The starting point of these discussions is the system now in use—the kind of international money we work with at present. This money is, of course, any international medium of exchange for settling accounts between residents of different countries. The world has used one such means—gold—for centuries. Secret Agent James Bond, as he set off in search of Goldfinger, had a top secret briefing in basic economics from the Bank of England. As his creator, Ian Fleming, put it: "The great thing to remember about gold is that it's the most valuable and most easily marketable commodity in the world. You can go into any town in the world, almost any village, and hand over a piece of gold and get goods or services in exchange."

The world's governments—Communist and non-Communist alike—recognize this, try to capitalize on it, try to control the ownership of gold because of it. A transfer of gold is the classic way for a nation to pay its debts in global transactions. And a country is called upon to make such transfers when its citizens buy more from abroad than they are able to earn by their exports. In assessing a nation's currency and judging its international stand-

(a) five French francs, (b) one Russian silver ruble, (c) a Swiss five franc piece, (d) one West German mark, (e) one East German mark, (f) one thousand Italian lire, and (g) a Pakistani five paisa coin.

g

ing, economists look at that country's balance of payments—that is, how its payments for imports are covered by its income from exports. Other factors enter the picture —loans, foreign investments, tourist travel, the cost of shipping, and even the stationing of troops overseas. These are sometimes called "invisible" exports or imports. But the first fundamental concern of any nation is its balance of trade—whether exports are keeping up with imports.

Take the mythical land of Madrilena, somewhere south of the equator, as an example. One year it might sell 100 million dollars' worth of cocoa and peanuts abroad. If it bought, in the same year, 110 million dollars' worth of tractors, transistor radios, and automobiles from other countries, it would have a foreign exchange deficit of 10 million dollars. In one form or another, this would mean 10 million dollars' worth of its currency in the hands of foreigners who did not want to spend it within the country, but wanted instead to convert it into a currency they could spend elsewhere. Madrilena's banks could, of course, settle the matter quickly by transferring gold to those countries that had sold it the additional $10 million of imports. Or its banks could make the payments from any holdings they might have of dollars, Swiss francs, pounds sterling, or other "hard" currencies—so called because they are widely acceptable in world trade. Or its government might borrow either gold or these hard currencies from a foreign government, a foreign bank, or an international institution.

Such balance-of-payments deficits as that of Madrilena

are common enough. In any one year half the countries of the world may have them, while the other half has surpluses to match. The United States, which used to have only surpluses, has just experienced a decade of deficits—and acquired some new and illuminating experiences as a result. Developing countries—the old and new emerging nations of Africa, Asia, and Latin America—frequently have deficits. They need to import expensive machinery, trucks, bulldozers, tractors, and the like—long-lasting capital goods—to build up their industries and farms. They must pay with exports that consist mainly of farm products—cotton, coconuts, cocoa, coffee—things that are both quickly consumed and subject to price fluctuations, keen competition, changes in demand.

What happens when a country runs a chronic deficit? It simply goes deeper into debt. As it does so, every time a foreigner finds himself with a Madrilena peso in his pocket, he wants to get rid of it as fast as possible. This means Madrilena's banks are soon stripped of all gold and hard currencies. Or else the government puts limitations on the conversion of its money into other kinds of money. This may mean that a prospective importer has to get a government license before he can buy something abroad; it almost certainly will mean that he will have to fill out forms and get government permission to convert his pesos into foreign exchange to pay for the imported goods. Travelers from Madrilena will only be allowed to convert so many pesos when they leave the country. And as likely as not, there will then develop a black market in Madrilena pesos. People, both inside and outside the country, will be willing to sell pesos cheaper than at the official rates in order to turn them into a currency that *is* convertible into gold. Madrilena can make this practice illegal within its territory, but it can't do much about a bank just across its border that buys and sells pesos at what the market says they are worth.

When such a black market exists, official devaluation of the currency becomes a real possibility. Devaluation means making the currency cheaper in terms of gold or in terms of other currencies that maintain *their* ratio to gold. The British pound sterling, for instance, was worth about $4 until 1949 when one of recent history's most significant devaluations took place. The value of the pound was officially lowered to $2.80; some twenty other currencies linked to the pound, from the Icelandic crown to the Indian rupee, were all devalued by the same percentage.

A typical modern devaluation was carried out by Yugoslavia in 1965. Although a Communist country, Yugoslavia had been moving toward a free market internal economy since 1950 and has increased its foreign trade by allowing individual enterprises to export and import. By 1965 imports were outpacing exports so that Yugoslavia had a serious balance-of-payments deficit. By early 1965 tourists coming into the country were buying their dinars outside the country at 1,000 to 1,200 to the dollar

(a) a Yugoslavian dinar, (b) an Indian anna, (c) an Icelandic crown, and (d) a British one pound note.

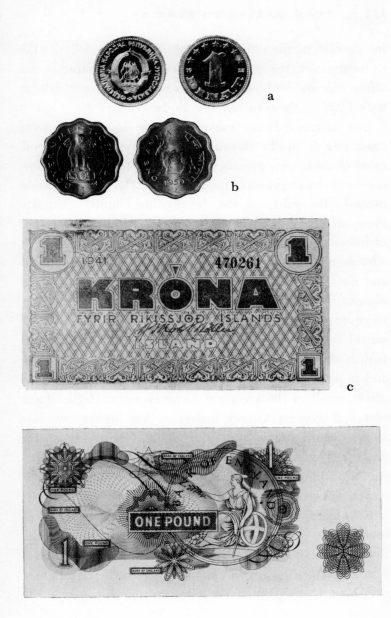

a

b

c

d

in contrast to the official rate of 750 to the dollar. And so by summer, the government decreed devaluation—the dinar was suddenly worth less since at the new rate it took 1,250 of them to buy one dollar.

Devaluation always makes imports more expensive, since people in the devaluating country have to spend more of their own currency to buy the foreign exchange needed to meet prices of goods abroad. Devaluation tends to make the prices of the devaluating country's exports more attractive because they become cheaper in terms of foreign currencies. Thus devaluation is a corrective to a balance-of-payments deficit—it should cut down imports and raise exports. In fact, these corrective forces are not necessarily as automatic as this. Once devaluation occurs there may be price changes at home and abroad that cancel out some of the effects. For instance, after the British devaluation in 1949, the price of imported food and imported raw materials went up within Britain as a direct result of the changed currency rates. Higher food costs led workers to seek higher wages; higher raw materials meant higher costs for many British export industries; therefore the price of British exports tended to rise, nullifying some of the competitive advantage of the currency reform.

Devaluation is one of the techniques a country can use to sell more goods than its rivals. But if one country can devalue so can another; and devaluation in one place can set off devaluation elsewhere, along with other retaliatory measures. During the 1930's many nations engaged in tit-for-tat tactics with their currencies, their tariffs, and other restrictions on imports. It amounted to a kind of trade war in which each tried to gain but all tended to lose, because the steps they took had the net effect of reducing the total volume of world trade.

Many people think that Hitler, Mussolini, and Japanese expansionism might never have become such destructive forces if it had not been for the economic muddle the world got itself into during the Depression. And on this basis, some of the leaders of the allied nations in World War II resolved to take measures to avoid the same kind of economic nationalism from recurring. Their representatives met at Bretton Woods, New Hampshire, in July 1944, and drew up the basic agreements founding two new international institutions that began operating as specialized agencies of the United Nations, in 1946, with forty-four nations.

John Maynard Keynes—by this time Lord Keynes— was one of the leading architects of the two institutions. They were the International Bank for Rehabilitation and Development, much better known today as the World Bank, and the International Monetary Fund. The World Bank has had notable success in financing dams, power stations, railroads, steel mills, highways, and harbors from the Snowy Mountains of Australia to the jungles of Thailand and the Congo, from Argentina and Austria to northern Norway. The International Monetary Fund has a less spectacular record as far as producing tangible economic results. But it plays an influential, even crucial, role in the realm of international money. It has helped rescue whole nations at the point of bankruptcy—rescued them in the sense it has kept them from being forced into measures harmful to the trade of their neighbors, measures which would have been likely to set off countermeasures starting a chain reaction detrimental to the international community as a whole.

Member nations of the fund are committed to declare and maintain a par value for their currency. This par value is stated either in terms of gold or in U.S. dollars

J. M. Keynes, Chairman of the United Kingdom delegation, confers with M. S. Stepanov of the U.S.S.R. and Vladimir Rybar of Yugoslavia at the international monetary conference held at Bretton Woods, New Hampshire, in 1944.

at a specified gold content (the two amount to the same thing). They agree not to change these par values except according to certain rules. They also agreed that after an initial postwar transition period they would allow their currencies to be converted into other currencies for the purposes of current trade, although not necessarily for longer-term capital transactions.

The fund itself is a mechanism designed to help its member countries keep these argreements, and thus allow stability and orderly change. Reduced to its basic essentials, it is a pool, or as its name states, a fund of gold and national currencies. The pool was created by having each member deposit a quota of gold and an additional amount of its own currency—the amount varying according to the member's national income. The countries have a right to draw, or borrow, foreign currencies from this fund. They can borrow without question the amount of their gold contribution—in IMF language, their gold *tranche*, after the French word for slice; after that they have to meet the conditions set by the other member countries. Usually these conditions require the borrowing nation to correct the situations that originally led to its economic difficulties.

The fund is an organization run by its members, and not a very democratic one. Each nation has a vote equivalent to the size of its quota. The United States, whose quota is by far the largest, has the most votes. The logic behind this weighted voting is very simple. If the countries with the least stake in the system, the least to lose, were able to outvote those with the most money involved, the fund might wind up with debts and no real assets.

By the 1960's, the fund had more than one hundred members. The Soviet Union, Communist China, and most other Communist countries were not members, presumably because the idea of cooperating so closely with capitalist countries and helping them out of economic difficulties is too radical a departure from official Communist ideology.

The International Monetary Fund is just one part, although an important part, of the monetary arrangements that allow travelers and businessmen to buy and sell freely and change their money in most of the industrialized parts of the world. There are other organizations and arrangements—some highly technical, complicated, and even mysterious.

There is within the ranks of the IMF a loosely related organization that calls itself "the Group of Ten," often referred to by journalists as "the Paris club." These are ten of the richest countries of the world which, in the early 1960's, decided that the resources of the fund might not be sufficient to meet all emergencies. They agreed to be prepared to hold billions of dollars worth of additional reserves ready for any serious drain on one or another of the world's key currencies. The Ten are: the United States, Britain, France, Federal Germany, Italy, Sweden, Belgium, the Netherlands, Canada, and Japan. An eleventh country, Switzerland, participates with the group on special terms.

Another important cog in present world monetary arrangements is the Bank for International Settlements in Basle, Switzerland. The BIS, as it is often called, was a forerunner of the International Monetary Fund and a pioneer in its field. It was established in 1930 to administer the World War I system of reparations and debt repayments. But even when this function became academic, because of massive failure to pay on the part of the debtor countries, the bank lingered on. It had proved itself useful enough to take part in some of the most complex international financial transactions of the next three and one-half chaotic decades. The bank is far removed from the public. It is run by officials of the central banks of member countries. It is one step higher than a banker's bank: it is a bank *for* banker's banks. It keeps its accounts in its own kind of gold francs, that is, a unit equivalent to the gold-backed Swiss franc of 1930. Since the devaluation of the Swiss franc in 1936, the BIS franc doesn't exist except on its books.

Although countries like Japan and the United States were once BIS members, they now participate on a special basis and the bank itself is a European institution. Its closed meetings on the second Monday of each month— except in August and September—bring together most of the governors of the central banks of Europe in Basle. The public gets a look at their work once a year, when the BIS issues its influential annual report assessing world economic conditions, showing who holds how much gold, weighing the value of different national currencies and expressing concern for international liquidity.

In recent years members of the International Monetary

Fund, the Bank for International Settlements, and the Paris Ten have been talking about something called a "possible shortage of international liquidity." They are even holding world meetings about it. A shortage of liquidity is the economists' way of describing a very common complaint—no money. Liquidity is cash, the means of making immediate payment. It may include credit if the borrower's credit is good, but if he has to stop and haggle about it, meet conditions and raise collateral, he isn't very liquid.

The bankers, cautious people that they are, have been talking about a *possible* shortage of international liquidity. There's no shortage now, they have said, but there might be, and we ought to do something about it before the situation becomes serious. World trade has been growing tremendously—from an annual $60 billion in 1950 to about $165 billion at the current (1965) level. And the amount of international money, the means of making instant payment, hasn't increased nearly as much.

How did this happen? And why the new need to do something about it? The answers can be found in the story of the United States dollar throughout the postwar era. During and after World War II the United States sent arms, planes, jeeps, food, medicine, bulldozers, and machinery abroad in vast quantities. Despite the fact that much of this material was given free of charge or subject to payment on long-term loans, including wartime lend-lease and the postwar Marshall Plan, some of the goods were paid for promptly and with cash. Since America had what war stricken countries wanted, they inevitably bought more from us than they sold; the other countries in the 1940's never seemed to be able to sell enough goods to us to earn the dollars they needed; there was a world-wide "dollar shortage." And we either accepted promises to pay or in some measure received gold. Gold accumulated at Fort Knox, Kentucky, and at the United States Assay Office and the Federal Reserve Bank of New York near the tip of downtown Manhattan. We had $24.5 billion worth of it in 1949—about two-thirds of the world's total gold used for monetary purposes.

But by the 1950's a reversal in our balance-of-payments took place. The Western European countries made rapid recoveries. They were selling more of their goods and services to each other, to the United States, and to the rest of the world. The dollar shortage was over. The United States still sold more "visible" *goods*—wheat, cotton, tobacco, automobiles, and other hardware—than it bought. But it started running up debts in other ways, in what the economists sometimes call the "invisible" items. For instance, American companies were sending investment dollars abroad to build and equip factories for their subsidiaries in foreign countries. American tourists went abroad, spending dollars in far greater number than the tourists who came to our shores. Then there were the U.S. troops kept abroad on duty around the world—in West Germany and other NATO countries, in Vietnam, and elsewhere. They converted their pay in dollars into marks, lire, and other currencies as they bought things abroad. And they were housed and fed through the expenditure of foreign moneys bought with dollars. All of these were debit items in our balance-of-payments.

At first these debits were regarded as normal and healthy. They meant that other countries were earning enough to be able to repay their own past debts. But by the late 1950's the size and persistence of the American international deficits began to be alarming. President

The Federal Reserve Bank of New York near the tip of downtown Manhattan; the head office of the Chase Manhattan Bank can be seen across the street.

Eisenhower, toward the end of his second term, voiced concern. We were spending $1, $2, $3, and even $4 billion more a year than we were earning. As this vast store of dollars was put into foreign hands, some of them were being cashed in at the U.S. Treasury for gold. And this loss of gold prevailed through the first half of the 1960's under Presidents Kennedy and Johnson. By early 1967 the United States gold stocks had slumped from their $24.5 billion high to about $13 billion.

By itself, this gold drain, large as it was, did not mean a crisis. Our gold stock still represented about one-third of the world's total monetary gold stocks, which are estimated in the neighborhood of $41 to $43 billion. At this point the U.S. gold holding was about one-half the amount of dollars and other short-term claims against dollars in foreign hands. Considering the state of the economy, and the amounts of money owed on a long-term basis by foreigners the dollar was still—in the words of Treasury Secretary Henry Fowler—"the strongest currency in the world." But the reduced state of American reserves was plainly worrisome from the international monetary point of view. Worrisome enough for bankers and trade experts to dream nightmares of a new international depression, with idle ships, stores of unsold grain, silent factories, and capped oil wells. Their thinking ran this way: Suppose the American gold drain were to continue, and the run on the bank began. Wouldn't there be much less money available of the kind that has been internationally acceptable? And might not this contrac-

tion in the world's money supply lead to a trade crisis—
a widespread inability to pay for the goods of other countries and a consequent sharp curtailment of foreign commerce almost everywhere?

The strength of the American dollar and the size of the
U.S. gold stock are important to the rest of the world because the dollar has become a *reserve* currency. That
pledge to buy gold at $35 per ounce, and sell it at that
price—a pledge repeated by a succession of presidents—
makes the dollar "as good as gold." When the United
States held two-thirds of the world's monetary gold, the
soundness of the dollar, and its redeemability in gold, was
unquestioned. Dollars could be used for transactions between Venezuelans and Italians, Turks and Yugoslavs,
Africans and Pakistanis. Central banks of different countries could use them to buy any needed currency to settle
trade deficits. And so, these central banks, when they had
a surplus of dollars as the result of favorable trade balance,
hung on to them—kept them as reserves against the day
they would have to pay them out. Dollars, as well as gold,
could be used to back other national currencies. This was
not a new development, by the way. The British pound
had been serving in this role for decades and has continued to do so among many countries, despite some difficulties in the 1940's and 1960's. The French franc, too,
has become a reserve currency of some standing. But the
dollar, in the postwar world, has led the list.

Can it remain on top? A serious further decline in
American gold stocks would start bankers and traders

looking for a way of switching their reserves out of dollars and into something safer—which means, of course, gold itself. And instead of having gold-plus-dollars as a means of making international payments, the world would find itself with only gold.

The world's supply of gold has not grown fast enough to provide the kind of expansion the international community needs. About $1.2 to $1.4 billions of new gold was mined in the free world in each of the five years 1960 through 1964. Gold sales by the Soviet Union, a fairly important gold-producing country, added several million dollars worth a year. Less than one-half of this supply of new gold found its way into the national treasuries of different nations for use as money, or backing for money. Of course, each year some gold goes into jewelry, dental work, and specialized industrial products and tools. But by far the biggest part of the unofficial stores of gold seems to be in the hands of hoarders—people who don't trust one currency or another, people who think that if they accumulate gold it will some day bring them more than the $35 per ounce it is now worth. There are, by their actions, speculating that the dollar—and other currencies linked to it—will be devalued and that gold will some day be worth more—$40, $50, or $70 per ounce. They are betting this way despite the repeated assurances by Presidents and Secretaries of the Treasury that no such devaluation is in prospect.

It costs the hoarder something to speculate against the dollar, the pound, or the franc. He gets no interest on gold; it is a singularly unproductive metal. If he is a citizen of a country where private gold stocks are allowed, he will probably pay a bank to hold it for him to ensure its safety. American citizens, by law, are not allowed to hold monetary gold. Most other countries have similar restrictions. Obviously, a lot of gold is hoarded illegally, in bars, sheets, and coins, at some risk to the owners. The gold hoarder knows all these disadvantages, but he also knows that in today's world, the price of gold is not likely to go down, and for this reason he clings to his yellow metal.

No one knows how large the total private holdings are. Some estimates put them as high as $15 to $17 billion, higher than the official holdings of the United States and well over one-third of the world's official holdings.

Hoarding gold is a tradition in some countries. French farmers, among others, have had a habit of stuffing gold coins into their mattresses. An Indian bride, no matter how poor, must have some gold in her dowry, and this has meant the smuggling of millions of dollars into India despite New Delhi's official desire to control its own monetary system.

Gold is traded officially, in keeping with the laws of the land, in a number of different centers. London, Paris, Zurich, and Beirut are all important gold markets. London is the market place for the output of South Africa's mines—the most important in the world. New deposits discovered in the 1950's boosted production to almost 30 million ounces in 1964—approximately 720 million dollars or close to three-fourths of free world output. The

Soviet Union sells some of its gold in London, some in Paris and Switzerland. Soviet output is a state secret. It was once regarded as rivaling South Africa's, but new evidence in the 1960's indicates it is much smaller. Soviet gold sales averaged about $250 million annually from 1957 to 1962, and then jumped to $550 and $450 million in 1963 and 1964 to help pay for a billion dollars worth of grain bought from the West to make up for a disastrous harvest in 1963. At the time of purchases, the Central Intelligence Agency, foregoing its customary secrecy, made public its estimate that Soviet gold reserves were about $2 billion—considerably less than what many western estimates had been. The implication was that the wheat purchases were a significant drain on Russian gold stocks. The Soviet news agency denied that the country's reserves were depleted. However, Soviet sources have reported new and concerted efforts to increase gold production and Soviet officials act as though they, too, are worried about their gold drain.

Monetary gold is usually fashioned into bars slightly smaller than the average brick and a good deal heavier—twenty-seven pounds—that are worth about $14,000 each. London gold merchants say they often have orders for small flat pieces weighing slightly less than four ounces and worth about $125 each, which obviously can be slipped into a vest pocket or sewn into the lining of a coat. In Japan not too long ago police seized a shipment of women's corsets with seventy-two of these morsels of gold tucked away in them. When central banks are paying off their debts, legally and openly, the gold may not even leave the building where it has been stored; it may simply go to another room with another label of ownership on it. The Federal Reserve Bank of New York has vaults five stories below street level in downtown Manhattan, which have held as much as $13 billion dollars worth of gold for *other* governments simply because it is cheaper and considered safer to keep it there.

The French, however, have taken exception to this pattern. In 1965, the story goes, President de Gaulle said pointedly to one of his banking officials that he would not like to be responsible for the security of the national treasure if it were so far from home. And thereafter, gold for the Bank of France began to leave New York for Paris in secret well-secured voyages, sometimes by air, sometimes by sea.

General de Gaulle also startled the world early in 1965, when, at one of his news conferences, he indicated his recipe for international monetary reform. He made clear that he foresees the end of the dollar's supremacy as a reserve currency and wants more stress on gold. "There can be no other criterion, no other standard than gold," he said. "Yes, gold which never changes, which can be shaped into ingots, bars, coins, which has no nationality and which is eternally and universally accepted as the unalterable fiduciary value par excellence."

The General's views were thought to reflect the thinking of Jacques Rueff, a French economist, who believes that a fixed price for gold is undersirable, that currencies

The Federal Reserve Bank of New York vaults have held up to $13 billion worth of gold for other governments.

should be allowed to fluctuate freely in their relationship to gold. And he also suggested that, as a starter for this fluctuation, the price of gold should be doubled, from $35 to $70 per ounce. In other words, that the dollar be devalued by half.

This proposal is only one of the many—and as far as American officials go, probably the most undersirable—

that have been offered to solve the international liquidity problem. Americans say the Rueff proposal would just make things worse, because one devaluation, following continual pledges to the contrary, would undermine confidence in the dollar and lead to more hoarding and further contraction of the lesser international money supply.

Some of the other proposals are equally important and interesting. Professor Robert Triffin of Yale University wants to transform the International Monetary Fund into a world central bank with the power of issuing an international money. Several other suggestions call for the creation of a "composite reserve unit," sometimes referred to as a *cru*, which would be backed by the currencies of a number of the industrial countries. This would help relieve the dollar of its primary responsibility and put greater reliance on currencies like the German Deutsche Mark and the French and Swiss francs which have strong reserves. But how such a unit is to be established and, above all, who is to control what are the key questions that the experts have not yet agreed on.

All these proposals are still being mulled over. The IMF meeting in Washington during 1965 set up a timetable of world monetary meetings which continued through 1966 and into 1967—carrying forward the debate on international liquidity and the question of a world money.

INDEX

INDEX